WANTED
IN INDIANA

WANTED IN INDIANA

INFAMOUS HOOSIER FUGITIVES

Andrew E. Stoner

THE History PRESS

Published by The History Press
Charleston, SC
www.historypress.com

First published 2021

Manufactured in the United States

ISBN 9781467147309

Library of Congress Control Number: 2020948632

Notice: The information in this book is true and complete to the best of our knowledge. It is offered without guarantee on the part of the author or The History Press. The author and The History Press disclaim all liability in connection with the use of this book.

CONTENTS

ACKNOWLEDGEMENTS

The author gratefully acknowledges the support of the following in the preparation of this work: John Rodrigue, Hayley Behal, Anna Burrous and The History Press and Arcadia Publishing; Steven L. Polston, Jerry Miller, John Maxwell and Randolph Scott; Ron Hoke and Jeff Keim of Goshen Historical Society; Ray Boomhower of the Indiana Historical Society; Sherlyn L. Hayes-Zorn of the Nevada Historical Society; John Harris and the Indiana Album; Kelly Lippie of the Tippecanoe County Historical Association; and Keenan Salla of the Indiana State Archives.

INTRODUCTION

In the summer and fall of 1970, pop radio stations across the nation (most of them on the AM dial) were offering up a catchy song, "Indiana Wants Me," complete with police sirens and gunfire, reflecting the deadly end for a Hoosier fugitive.

Written, sung and produced by R. Dean Taylor, a Toronto native, the song tells the story of a young man on the run after killing someone in Indiana for insulting his girl. Taylor said he wrote it after watching the Academy Award–nominated 1967 film *Bonnie and Clyde*, and it scored his first—and only—hit on the charts.

While Bonnie Parker and Clyde Barrow weren't Indiana fugitives, in their same era the state *had* produced the nation's first Public Enemy No. 1 in John Dillinger. Dillinger's criminal exploits were well known by the time "Indiana Wants Me" became a hit, and unfortunately, Indiana provided many other "notable" fugitives who would leave their own marks.

"Indiana Wants Me" was produced by a new record label, Rare Earth, a project of Motown impresario Barry Gordy Jr., and peaked at number 5 on the Billboard Top 100 list on November 7, 1970. It landed on *Cashbox* magazine's Top 100 Singles for the week of November 14, 1970, and for the year, "Indiana Wants Me" ended up number 54 on the Top 100 songs of 1970, as measured by *Billboard* magazine, and remained on the charts for fifteen weeks.

There were—and are—haters of the song. Author Tom Reynolds included "Indiana Wants Me" on his list of the 52 Most Depressing Songs You've

Ever Heard.[1] Another critic called the song "God-awful," and humorist David Sedaris had some fun remembering the song from his suburban 1970s youth, noting his admiration of the song was met with "an absence of agreement I can only describe as deafening."[2]

What is clear is that Indiana fugitives who've declared, "Lord, I can't go back there" have meant those words with a vengeance—such as two Lafayette youth who murdered the Tippecanoe County sheriff's deputies who were transporting them to prison; a series of troubling breakouts from the venerable (but not escape proof) Indiana State Prison in Michigan City; a gun-toting Elwood "girl" who was a favorite of newspaper reporters throughout the 1930s and '40s; diamond thieves; a young married couple who turn into robbers while on their honeymoon; fugitives who eluded capture for more than twenty years; a seventeen-year-old Indiana fugitive executed by the state of Nevada; and even a fugitive who became a Kentucky cop while on the run from Indiana.

In the modern era, spree killers driven by insatiable drug habits and vicious sexual predators emerged, with Indiana producing the very first fugitive profiled (and captured) via the popular television show *America's Most Wanted.*

The stories here examine not only the trail of destruction criminals have left in their wake but also their lives on the run. In the end, either through hard work by police or death, Indiana fugitives have answered to the rule of law in all eras.

1

1920-29

TOO FAT TO BE A FUGITIVE?

Fugitive(s): Edward Stevens and Arthur Welling
Wanted For: April 11, 1920, safe robbery, Indianapolis, Indiana
July 4, 1920, escape, Marion County Jail, Indianapolis, Indiana
Captured: Stevens, June 8, 1921, Carlinville, Illinois
Welling, December 11, 1921, San Francisco, California

Twenty-four inmates at the Marion County Jail in Indianapolis took the term *Independence Day* literally on July 4, 1920, and successfully escaped the aging jail as the sheriff slept.

One man who did not escape, Edward Stevens, was only left behind because the space left over after his cell bars were sawed through was too small for the big man to fit through. Twenty-four others had no problems getting out, including Stevens's partner in crime, Arthur Welling. Both Stevens and Welling had been indicted for using nitroglycerin and dynamite caps to blow open the safe of a filling station at Twenty-Fifth and Meridian Streets on April 11, 1920.

The two men were arrested shortly after the safe was blown and its contents of more than $2,000 was lifted. The *Indianapolis Star* reported, "The robbery is one of the 'neatest jobs' in Indianapolis in many months. The character of the work, they [police detectives] said, indicated clearly that it was done by professionals." Police said the safe was blown by pouring a charge of nitroglycerine into two holes drilled into the door of the safe. The explosion was so precise, police reported, that no other parts of the filling station office were damaged or disturbed.[3] Six days later, detectives, acting on a tip, arrested Stevens and Welling at the Severin Hotel in downtown Indianapolis, and they were housed on the second floor of the Marion County Jail, known as "U.S. row," usually reserved for federal inmates.

On May 16, 1920, the sheriff announced that he had interrupted a large escape scheme believed to be masterminded by some of the twenty-five federal prisoners. Four hack saws were found smuggled into the jail inside a loaf of bread, which had been sent to the jail for one of the prisoners. "The bread, a dozen rolls and a two-layer cake were delivered at the jail Sunday noon by a boy, thought to have been a Western Union messenger, and were to be given to Ollie Brown, a taxicab driver, who is held on a charge of manslaughter." The baked goods touched off suspicion when a deputy noted a thumb print on one end of the bread, as well as cigarette papers visible between the layers of the cake.[4]

The federal inmates had been given opportunities to leave their cells during the day and were permitted to exercise in the corridors, and Sheriff Robert F. Miller believed they planned to use the saws to cut the bars of the outside windows of the jail. Miller said that he attempted to learn from Western Union who had sent the baked goods to the jail, but there was no record of it there. Sheriff Miller seemed satisfied that he had thwarted any attempts to escape the jail—that was until July 4, when two dozen of his captives walked away unmolested. A jailer on the second floor, where the men were housed, was knocked on the head, gagged and tied up in order to assist in the getaway.

"The wholesale jail delivery was not discovered until nearly an hour later, and then only by the accidental capture of two of the fugitives by [other] police officers who were investigating a downtown mugging," the *Indianapolis Star* reported. "The men confessed that they had escaped from jail and the policemen notified police headquarters, who sent an officer to the jail to rouse Sheriff Miller from his sleep." Stevens was one of the only men who remained on the nearly deserted second floor of the jail. "Two bars of his cell were sawed, but he is a big man and was unable to squeeze through the narrow opening to freedom," the *Star* reported.[5]

In the days and weeks that followed, most of the twenty-four escapees were rounded up and returned to the jail, with the exception of Welling, who remained at large. His partner, Stevens, decided on a new tact to exit the jail by posting a large $5,000 bond to win his release until trial. His release, however, was thwarted on the steps of the jail as he attempted to depart with his attorney. Waiting there for him was a Shelby County sheriff's deputy, who promptly arrested him on a separate larceny charge pending against him.[6] Allegedly backed by wealthy Chicago crime figures, Stevens promptly posted a second bond in Shelby County and was set free—and intended to stay so.

Stevens subsequently failed to show up for numerous court hearings scheduled—and rescheduled. His attorney and bail bondsmen repeatedly told the court that they expected Stevens to appear. He did not. Finally, in June 1921, police at Carlinville, Illinois, a small town about 250 miles southwest of Indianapolis, reported they had Stevens under arrest. Stevens did not resist efforts to return him to Indianapolis to face his old charges and new charges related to "jumping bond."[7]

While Stevens was back under arrest and preparing to face the charges against him for the safe blowing of the Indianapolis filling station, Welling remained elusive. Finally, on December 11, 1921, a year and a half after he had walked away from the Marion County Jail, Welling was reported captured at San Francisco, California.

San Francisco Police were holding Welling, thirty-seven, under the alias of "Frank Lynch," but he had been identified by means of a photograph and physical measurements to be Welling. Welling was also suspected of a safe robbery at the Argonaut Mineral Mine near Jackson, California. That heist reportedly netted him minerals valued at more than $45,000.[8]

While Welling's capture was big news back in Indianapolis, with the *Indianapolis Star* referring to him as a "master burglar," San Francisco newspapers were more interested in filling their pages with accounts of actor Fatty Arbuckle's trial for murder underway in that city. Sources told *Indianapolis Star* reporters that Welling was "one of the most expert criminals in the country" and praised his adeptness in the use of burglary tools and 'soap' to blow safes. "No job is said to have been too difficult for him to attempt."[9]

Indianapolis detectives were sent to San Francisco to retrieve Welling and held him handcuffed for the entire return trip, locked in a stateroom on the train, with one officer handcuffed to each of his hands. "Every legal effort was made to prevent the detectives from leaving California with the cracksman, and the officers had received tips to the effect that a gang, of which Welling is said to be a member, would attempt to take their prisoners from them by force if the officers relaxed their vigilance sufficiently to give the thieves an opportunity," the *Indianapolis Star* reported.[10]

News reports made it clear that police and prosecutors in California were opposed to releasing Welling to Indiana authorities. The Indianapolis detectives apparently took the opportunity of a break in the legal proceedings to keep Welling in California to quickly escort him to the train and depart for the east.

Despite all the wrangling, Welling's fate was determined rather quickly on February 5, 1922, just two weeks after returning to Indianapolis. He pleaded guilty to a charge of unlawful use of explosives and was sentenced to two to fourteen years in the state prison. The hefty Stevens, who also had decided earlier to plead guilty to various charges, was already at the state prison. Prosecutors had been unable to gain his cooperation, however, in giving a statement implicating Welling in their criminal activities.[11]

A LONG ROAD TO JUSTICE FOR DREYFUS RHODES

Fugitive(s): Dreyfus Rhodes
Wanted For: January 8, 1925, escape, Oklahoma State Penitentiary, McAlester, Oklahoma
April 1, 1926, murder of police officer in Vincennes, Indiana
October 2, 1927, escape, Knox County Jail, Vincennes, Indiana
Captured: August 17, 1928, Oak Creek, Colorado

It took a decade to complete, but the long and sometimes complicated road to justice for fugitive Dreyfus Rhodes finally came to an end. Rhodes, a native of tiny Porum, Oklahoma, in Muskogee County, started his life of crime early at the age of sixteen in 1916. His life ended uneventfully inside a cell at the Indiana State Prison, his name long forgotten as an Indiana (and Oklahoma) fugitive.

Rhodes became an Indiana fugitive while he was on the run from Oklahoma when he shot and killed a Vincennes police officer on April 1, 1926, a little over a year after he escaped an Oklahoma prison.

Rhodes and two other men, including bank robber W.E. Collingsworth (known as the "Houdini of Oklahoma"), fled the state penitentiary in McAlester, Oklahoma, on January 8, 1925. Running east through Arkansas, Missouri, Illinois and eventually to Vincennes, Indiana, he brought violence with him as he attempted to stay out of the clutches of police. "All extra guards with bloodhounds were searching Pittsburg County [Oklahoma] early Friday for three convicts who escaped after throwing the state penitentiary into darkness for several minutes," the *Daily Oklahoman* reported. "The escape occurred shortly after dark when a wire leading into the penitentiary, which also connects with charged wires on top of the prison wall, had been 'shorted,' the escape was made."[12]

It was believed that Rhodes and his accomplices successfully figured out how to darken the prison, at least temporarily. "Pandemonium reigned when the lights went off," one report indicated. "Prisoners banged on bars, others who did not wish to escape, remained in their tracks, fearing for their lives if they moved.…As soon as the lights winked out, guards on the walls began firing their guns, and this it is believed, kept others within the walls."[13]

From January 1925 to April 1926, Rhodes eluded capture but fell on hard luck as he tried to get change for a fake five-dollar bill at the Palace of Sweets candy store on Main Street in Vincennes. The shop owner notified police, who arrived and quickly engaged in a gun battle. One of the officers, Simon A. Carey, was wounded in the abdomen and died later at a local hospital.

"An unidentified bandit was shot through the head in a revolver fight between two bandits and three policemen on Main Street at Noon," the *Indianapolis News* reported.[14]

While one of the men shooting it out with the police was wounded, Rhodes got away by fleeing in a nearby automobile. A posse of 150 men was quickly formed to try to find Rhodes, "who is reported to be armed with two pistols and plenty of ammunition…and will likely try to shoot himself out of a trap." Five days after the shooting, detectives tracked Rhodes down to a house at Bicknell, Indiana. He and Albert King, injured in the shootout, were both charged with murder for the death of Officer Carey.[15]

A day after his arrest, Rhodes told Knox County judge Thomas B. Coulter that he would plead guilty to the murder, and the judge summarily sentenced him to death—all within a week of the shooting incident. The judge scheduled Rhodes to be electrocuted on July 19. The swift nature of the case—including sentencing a defendant to death without the benefit of a trial—made national news.

Despite the speedy movement of his case, Rhodes apparently thought better of the matter after consulting with an attorney and successfully petitioned for a new trial. He won his bid for a second trial, scheduled to start on October 11, 1927, but apparently grew impatient. Nine days before the trial was to start, Rhodes escaped the Knox County Jail at Vincennes with the help of two local boys.

The sheriff said two boys, ages eleven and twelve, assisted Rhodes by giving him keys that allowed him to unlock his cell. The juveniles, also held at the county jail on other charges, escaped with Rhodes and made it as far as Louisville, Kentucky, before being captured. The sheriff explained that the two boys were receiving treatment at the county jail's hospital room when one obtained a set of cell keys. "In exchange for a pack of cigarettes, they agreed to obtain the keys for Rhodes and opened his cell, and escaped with him," INS reported.[16]

Knox County sheriff Henry Mack's prediction that Rhodes would head west was correct. Ten months later, in August 1928, Rhodes had the misfortune of trying to hide out in Oak Creek, Colorado, while a massive manhunt was underway for a bank robbery in the state that left four people dead. After briefly questioning him about the bank robbery, police cleared Rhodes of any involvement in the case but soon learned that he was a fugitive from Indiana.[17]

Back in Indiana, Rhodes's case was moved to Gibson County for the murder of Officer Carey. Rhodes was jailed at the Vanderburgh County Jail in Evansville, however, after concerns were raised that the jail at Princeton was no match for a man of Rhodes's skills. "The Gibson County Jail has been condemned as dilapidated and insecure," the *Princeton Daily Clarion* reported.[18]

Rhodes was found guilty of murdering the Vincennes police officer on November 18, 1928. As the verdict was announced, reporters noted that he remained "stoic and without the flicker of an eyelid, and without a change in his forced but steady smile." As before, Rhodes was sentenced to death.[19]

Throughout 1929, attorneys for Rhodes continued to successfully delay the scheduled execution, and in July 1930, the Indiana Supreme Court ruled that Rhodes was entitled to a new trial (his third) on the murder charge.[20] A third trial for Rhodes was conducted in January 1931 in Gibson County, and once again, he was found guilty but only of voluntary manslaughter, rather than murder. As a result, he successfully evaded the state's electric chair and instead was sentenced to twenty-one years in prison.[21]

With nothing left to lose, and his life spared, Rhodes gloated to officers transporting him to the state penitentiary that he had nearly escaped the Gibson County Jail while his third trial was underway. Rhodes said he used a piece of an old spoon and an iron brace from a cell cot to chisel out concrete next to the bars of his cell. Rhodes complained that he could have succeeded in escaping if given more time, but authorities were too quick in transporting him to the state prison at Michigan City.[22]

Unhappy at Michigan City, Rhodes unsuccessfully sought to have his sentence transferred to an Oklahoma prison in 1933. In 1936, he was denied a parole request. He died in prison before his sentence was complete.[23]

BEFORE DILLINGER, THERE WAS COUNT LUSTIG

Fugitive(s): Albert Grauman (Also Known as Count Victor Lustig)
Wanted For: April 6, 1927, escape, Lake County Jail, Crown Point, Indiana
Captured: September 28, 1935, New York City

The Lake County Jail at Crown Point, Indiana, housed perhaps the most famous Hoosier fugitive of all in the early 1930s: John Dillinger. However, it wasn't Dillinger but another colorful felon who first proved that the "escape proof" jail could be compromised and did so seven years earlier than Dillinger did.

A day after an unusually busy visitor's day at the jail on April 6, 1927, the Lake County sheriff had to embarrassingly admit that he had lost one of his charges. Thirty-nine-year-old con man Albert Grauman (whose birth name was Robert V. Miller) and two other inmates were missing. Grauman was visited at the jail a day before the breakout by his wife, who rode the train from her Chicago home. Jailers accused her of slipping her husband saw blades during her visit.

Grauman, who would become better known in subsequent years for one of his more colorful aliases, Count Victor Lustig, undertook the Crown Point escape as just one part of what turned out to be a lifetime of incredible feats of criminal activity.

Grauman, or Lustig, first caught the notice of police on a confidence charge in 1917 in St. Louis, followed soon by a vagrancy charge in Los Angeles in 1923, a larceny charge in San Francisco in 1925 and later acquittals for confidence game schemes in Fort Worth, Texas, and Miami, Florida, both in 1931.[24]

At the time of his escape at Crown Point, Lustig was wanted in Chicago and Seattle and Spokane, Washington. Indianapolis police had arrested him during a spending spree in that city after he and his brother were found to be selling envelopes filled with newspaper clippings, purporting to be Liberty Bonds. Not all of the bonds held by Lustig were bogus. When arrested, he was still in possession of several stolen Liberty Bonds, lifted earlier from a Gary real estate agent, Zen McNair, who told police Lustig had swindled him out of more than $10,000. Police also seized rollers, inking bonds, vials of chemicals, pens, brushes and blank paper for the making of fake bonds.[25]

Lustig was taken to Lake County to await trial on the theft charges brought by McNair. He lucked out to be housed at the jail while renovations were underway. In addition, jailers reported "scores of visitors called at the jail yesterday and attendants were kept busy during the visiting hours so that prisoners could not be given the usual close surveillance." Hammers and other tools being used by workers completing renovations on the jail were apparently also within reach of inmates.[26]

Escaping the Crown Point lock-up along with Lustig were fellow inmates identified as Red Weidner, twenty-three, and Leo Baugher, twenty-three, both suspect counterfeiters arrested on warrants held by the U.S. Secret Service.

"State and federal authorities today admitted that they were completely at sea in their search for three prisoners who escaped from the county jail yesterday morning after sawing two sets of steel bars," the *Gary Evening Times* reported. "Once out of their cells, the escapees used a blanket rope to climb from a jail window and disappeared as completely as though the earth had swallowed them." Lustig was described by reporters as "the tricky one of the three" who openly threatened other inmates to keep quiet while the steel bars were sawed.[27]

No witnesses reported seeing anything, no suspicious cars were noted near the jail or on the outskirts of town. Other jail inmates later reported that the sawing of bars started shortly after 8:30 p.m., when jailers declared "lights out," and continued throughout the night until the men finally gained their freedom around 4:30 a.m.

The manhunt went on for months, until public interest began to wane, and reporters turned to covering more recent crimes and incidents. Count Lustig, as he was now known, was back on the front pages, however, in October 1929, with the shocking news that he was under arrest in Paris, France, for using a fraudulent passport. His arrest there came complete with a later story that continued to grow in infamy that Lustig had successfully conned a group of French scrap metal businessmen into believing he was a high French government official authorized to "sell" the Eifel Tower, which during the era, was reported to have fallen into disrepair.[28]

While on the run from charges in Indiana (and several other states), Lustig had moved freely across the continent, European authorities said, living for short periods of time in England, Belgium, Germany and France. It wasn't until he entered France that questions were raised about the validity of his passport.

Lustig was eventually extradited to the United States at the princely sum of $694 to the taxpayers of Bristol County, Massachusetts. He was held there on a charge of larceny for swindling Thomas A. Kearnes of $42,000 in investment funds.[29] Released on "heavy bonds," on the Massachusetts charges, by February 1932, authorities there said they "held little hope" that Lustig and his accomplices would return to face trial for the charges.[30]

Back in Gary, McNair (who had posted a reward fund to help find Lustig) was told there were no county funds to pay to extradite Lustig to Indiana. If McNair wanted Lustig back to face charges, "he would have to pay the expenses incurred," the *Hammond Times* explained. "McNair did not seem to be very jubilant over the fugitive's arrest and expressed fear for his life saying that since Lustig's 1927 arrest, he had been approached and threatened by persons believed to be Lustig's confederates."[31]

Lustig's good luck eluding Indiana authorities continued, eventually set loose on local charges entered against him in Oklahoma and Missouri. He remained at large for another five years.[32]

In May 1935 came more screaming headlines in northwest Indiana, this time that "G men" had nabbed Lustig, operating again under the name Count Victor Lustig, in New York City with $52,000 in fake currency. New York police said they found the bogus bills in a Times Square subway station locker rented by Lustig. They also reported seizing a complete set of twenty steel plates for engraving $5, $10, $20 and $100 bills.[33]

The New York arrest by federal authorities was his twenty-ninth arrest overall, but somehow, Lustig had continuously avoided serving any significant jail time. One G man involved in arresting Lustig, who was not identified by reporters, noted, "He played up to his bogus title of count perfectly. He was distinguished looking, suave, and took every arterial advantage of his 45 years. He associated with respectable, unsuspecting persons, and went his way in a classy chauffeured car."

Lustig's arrest was big news in New York, with the *New York Daily News* labeling him "Swindler No. 1." Reporters noted, "For the first time in 27 years and 29 arrests, the government got the goods on the suave super-swindler, who speaks five languages, has Chesterfieldian manners, boasts a limousine and a chauffeur, and one of the wiliest rogues since Machiavelli."[34]

Incredibly, four months after Lustig was lodged in a federal jail in New York City, "mildly interested street loungers" watched as he slipped down a rope of bedsheets and fled" the jail.[35] The *New York Daily News* reported that Lustig impersonated a window cleaner to break free of "the grim bastille as more than a dozen watched him work without realizing they were seeing one of the world's few master criminals executing the masterpiece of his spectacular career."[36]

Lustig was seized twenty-seven days later and later convicted on various counterfeit charges in federal court in New York and sentenced to twenty years in prison to be served at Alcatraz Island. Prosecutors said that over the course of his career, Lustig had printed an estimated $2.3 million in fake money.[37] As late as 1947, federal authorities admitted portions of Lustig's phony bills were still being found in circulation across the United States.[38]

Lustig died in a federal prison hospital on March 11, 1947, at the age of fifty-seven. He was never tried on the charges lodged against him in Indiana.

DIAMONDS ARE A FUGITIVE'S BEST FRIEND

Fugitive(s): Lawrence L. Ghere and Rupert McDonald
Wanted For: May 17, 1926, murder, Indianapolis, Indiana
July 1927, bail skipping, Chicago, Illinois
Captured: Ghere, July 18, 1928, San Francisco, California
McDonald, August 17, 1928, Los Angeles, California

Diamonds and jewels were at the center of a long and far-reaching search for fugitives wanted for the murder of a prominent Indianapolis businessman.

On May 17, 1926, Wilkinson "Wilkie" Haag, forty-two, part owner of the Haag Drug Stores in Indianapolis, was "brutally slain" in a noonday robbery at the Green Mill Dance Gardens on East Thirty-Eighth Street in Indianapolis. "Haag was shot down after he refused to give a valuable diamond ring to two bandits who held him up in the lunchroom of the café," the *Indianapolis News* reported. After robbing Haag of fifty dollars in cash (but ignoring the cash drawer in the restaurant) and failing in their effort to get the ring—reported to be a five-and-a-half carat diamond in a gold setting—the bandits fled the scene in a Chrysler Roadster. "Police tightened the dragnet about the city and were running down every possible clew [sic]," the *News* added.[39]

Police understood immediately that Haag was the target of the robbery based on the eyewitness account of his female companion, identified as Jessie Murphy, twenty-eight, a bookkeeper at a local typewriter company, and a former beauty queen contest winner. She reported Haag, a married man, took her to lunch at the café. Murphy told police, "It was her custom to meet Haag about 1 p.m. each day and go for a ride or to some place for lunch.…The woman, although she was in a hysterical condition…gave a minute description of the two men who entered the restaurant."[40]

Murphy reported a Chrysler vehicle seemed to follow them to the restaurant and that the two men entered just moments after they were seated for lunch. Seated at the other end of the dining room, the men ordered soft drinks, and when the waiter left to get them, "the bandits drew revolvers and ordered the persons in the room to hold up their hands. One of the bandits then when into the kitchen and forced [the waiter] to come into the lunchroom and stand with his hands over his head." In Murphy's account, she told detectives that the men immediately demanded Haag's ring, but he refused to give it up. "We mean business," one of the men said to Haag and threatened to shoot him if he did not remove the ring.[41]

She said Haag was defiant, replying, "Be a man. Go ahead and shoot. You can't bluff me." The robber obliged and immediately shot Haag. "Haag staggered and would have fallen, but the other bandit struck him with a vicious blow with his fist and then kicked him through the open door. Haag fell on the ground outside and the larger of the two bandits fired a second time."[42]

Two men arriving at the restaurant to deliver ice told police that they saw the men riffling through Haag's pockets and then fleeing in a panic moments later. Murphy crawled under a table inside the restaurant and was not injured or robbed of any of the contents of her purse.

An autopsy showed that the second shot aimed at Haag while he lay prostrate on the ground was an apparent attempt to shoot off the third finger of his left hand to get the ring. The ring was recovered in the doorway of the café. "The second shot nearly severed the finger," the *News* reported. "The bullet, however, struck the gold band of the ring and broke it in two. The diamond was not damaged." Haag died from the first shot aimed at him, which tore through his abdomen from left to right and caused massive internal hemorrhaging.

The ring Haag was wearing continued to be the focus of a lot of attention. Murphy's mother, F.M. Murphy, while comforting her daughter in their near Eastside home, told a reporter, "I told Wilkie repeatedly that it was dangerous for him to wear that diamond all the time."[43] Haag's aunt, Lenora Haag, said her nephew greatly valued showing off the ring given to him by his uncle, Julius Haag, who along with Haag's father, William, founded the drug store company in 1876 and expanded it to multiple stores in the early 1900s. It was one of Indiana's first retail chains.[44]

Haag was known as a showy and flashy man. Apparently living at least partially as a bachelor (despite being married), the wealthy young man drove a nice car and dressed well. Haag's wife, Cora, reportedly lived in a separate downtown apartment building about a mile from her husband's downtown apartment. Reached by reporters after the news of her husband's death, Cora proved a colorful interview subject.

"He died like a man, the poor dear," she declared. She then quickly asked a reporter, "Did they get his diamond? He was always so fond of that ring. And did they take his automobile? He was fond of that car and got so much fun out of it in his way." Cora said she had not lived with Wilkie for about a year, "but we were the best of friends, and he would call me up two or three times a week. I have expected something like this, but if I could have talked to him before he went." As she spoke, "tears streamed down her face," and Cora said, "I can just imagine him daring those bandits to shoot. Oh, Wilkie, that was just like you. He was always headstrong and stubborn. Oh, those dogs, to shoot him and kick him after he was down. I wonder if he knew who they were?" Cora added, "Oh Wilkie, if things just could have been different. I tried every way, but I don't want to be drawn into this affair in any way." Her attention, it seems, turned again to the diamond ring, asking a reporter, "Where is his diamond now?"[45]

Miss Murphy continued to cooperate with investigators, including participating in at least two reenactments of the robbery, one at police headquarters and one at the scene of the shooting. She and another witness initially implicated a Lawrence man, Elmer McCormick, as one of the shooters. Police grilled McCormick and he participated in one of the reenactments, but he was later cleared.[46]

In the months that followed, police identified two men, Lawrence L. Ghere and Rupert McDonald (also known as Arthur C. McClelland), as their suspects. Both Ghere and McDonald were later held by Chicago police for the daring theft of diamonds and jewelry, valued at $500,000, from various jewelers at the famed Palmer House Hotel in Chicago.[47]

Indiana authorities made repeated attempts to extradite Ghere and McDonald to Indianapolis but were fought by Chicago authorities. They even took their key witness, Jessie Murphy, to Chicago to make a positive identification of the men, but Illinois authorities refused to relent and release him to Indiana.

The case against their suspects took a serious blow when Jessie Murphy, now thirty years old, died unexpectedly on January 15, 1928. She was in treatment for a variety of health issues, including a reported "nervous breakdown" after witnessing Haag's murder.

Despite protests from Indianapolis officials, a Chicago judge set a bond for Ghere and McDonald and released the two men from jail. Before Indianapolis police could arrest them on a murder warrant from Indiana, however, the two disappeared from bond.

That is how the matter remained until July 19, 1928, when a telegram arrived at the Indianapolis Police Department indicating Ghere and a man believed to be McDonald were both under arrest in San Francisco for the armed robbery of a malted milk company.

Under arrest, Ghere decided to "man up" and indicated that the other man arrested with him was not McDonald (later confirmed by a lack of a match of fingerprints) and agreed to talk to police if they would release the two women arrested with him. Described as two "cabaret entertainers from Chicago," the women had driven across country with Ghere and the other man a few weeks earlier.

"The women are innocent," Ghere told San Francisco police. "Let them go and I'll tell you something you want to know." He then confessed to the Chicago jewelry robberies but claimed he had only cleared $5,000 from the heists. He denied, however, any knowledge of the Haag murder in Indianapolis. Ghere agreed to be extradited to Illinois, he said, but not Indiana (where a murder charge was pending).[48]

To verify the identities of Ghere and the other man, Indianapolis police sent via air mail fingerprint records, photographs and Bertillon measurements (a system of measuring head length and breadth, length of a middle finger, length of the left foot and length of the cubit or forearm, popularized by French police expert Alphonse Bertillon, eventually supplanted by fingerprinting). The second man, Nelson Chittick, was reportedly McDonald's half-brother but was not the man wanted for the Haag murder.[49]

The second suspect, Rupert McDonald, was located in Los Angeles and arrested and vigorously fought his return to Indianapolis. He, like Ghere before him, eventually lost the extradition fight and was brought back later in August.[50]

McDonald was the first to go on trial, in March 1929, and witnesses dutifully identified him as the second, smaller man who had robbed Haag at the café. One of the witnesses, Elisha Chatman, said he witnessed the shooting and claimed it was Ghere who fired the second shot into Haag's body on the ground and McDonald who rifled through the dying man's pockets. "When we came up in front of the barbeque, I saw a man staggering at the west door…and I said 'That fellow must be drunk or hurt'….I saw the man with the gun stand right over Haag and shoot him in the side. Haag staggered out the door, and fell on his face on the gravel driveway."[51]

Chatman added that Ms. Murphy "was doing a lot of screaming and hollering. The only thing I could catch she was saying was, 'Wilkie, Wilkie!'" Chatman added, "I got some water and bathed Haag's face and head. I threw some of the water on Miss Murphy who had fainted and then I ran into the street and tried to stop some passing automobiles."[52]

McDonald was found guilty on a charge of murder on March 20, 1929, and was sentenced to life in prison. As Ghere's trial approached, speculation grew that he would take a plea and avoid a trial, and in fact he did. Ghere, too, received a life sentence on March 25, 1929. Both men sought clemency from the State Clemency Board in 1944, which recommended they be released after serving fifteen years behind bars.[53]

A DAPPER FUGITIVE SEEKING THE BIG TIME

Fugitive(s): Thomas O'Brien
Wanted For: March 29, 1926, murder and robbery, South Bend, Indiana
September 16, 1926, escape, Elkhart County Jail, Goshen, Indiana
Captured: January 23, 1927, Chicago, Illinois

If nothing else, Thomas O'Brien was an enterprising criminal, as he made not one but two attempts to break out of the Elkhart County Jail in Goshen—a quiet Indiana county seat town of less than ten thousand citizens—in both June and September 1926.

O'Brien—who made claims of having high-level criminal contacts that stretched from South Bend to Chicago to Salt Lake City to San Francisco—was unwilling to sit still while awaiting trial on a charge of murder. His second jail break attempt, during the early morning hours of September 16, 1926, allowed O'Brien and three others to slip out of the Goshen jail.

The *South Bend Tribune* reported that Elkhart County sheriff's deputies were searching areas along the Elkhart River bottoms, southwest of Goshen and along the Plymouth-Goshen trail. O'Brien was "pictured by police authorities from time to time as being affluent due to his reputed favor with certain women of the half world."[54]

To gain his escape, O'Brien, twenty-three, "sawed the padlock on the inner room of the cell provided for the desperate prisoners, and then two padlocks on the door opening into the 'bull pen' where other prisoners slept, were cut. At the outside of the 'bull pen,' he sawed a steel bar at the south window of the jail, another bar and two steal slates and through this opening the men escaped." Twenty-two other prisoners essentially had access to escape once all the bars were cut—sometime between 2:00 and 7:00 a.m.—but the space was too small for most to make a break. "As the bars were very close together officers believe most of the prisoners in the jail would have found it impossible to climb through," the *South Bend Tribune* reported. "Officers are of the opinion that those who did escape struggled for a long time to get through."[55]

One of the men who could not fit through the hole in the bars, John Hall, twenty-one, was O'Brien's partner on the robbery and murder charges that landed them in jail. The sheriff said Hall was "too stout" to fit through the bar openings. Perhaps frustrated by being left behind, Hall made a rather bold attempt to escape the jail a week after O'Brien successfully fled. Hall reached through the bars of his cell and grabbed the gun of a deputy sheriff who was escorting a woman into the cell block to visit her husband. He gave up, however, after being threatened with tear gas.[56]

South Bend officials, who wanted O'Brien and Hall for the robbery and murder of a drug store owner, were openly critical of Elkhart County sheriff Thomas Long for his handling of the case. The escape was the second one involving O'Brien (an earlier June attempt was thwarted), although four other prisoners (not including O'Brien) sawed through bars and escaped the jail on August 29—just two weeks before the current flight.

Authorities in neighboring St. Joseph County were also angry that O'Brien and Hall had successfully kept their cases in Elkhart County (where they were arrested on May 12, 1926, on a series of robbery and burglary charges). Their most serious crime, however, was the "spectacular daylight robbery" on March 29, 1926, at the Kriedler Pharmacy at 801 South Michigan Street in South Bend.

During that robbery, the store's owner, Louis C. Kriedler, fifty-three, walked in on O'Brien and Hall as they attempted to rob his store. Kriedler pulled a gun on the men and attempted to fire, but his gun would not fire. As he struggled to get his gun to work, the younger men took the weapon from Kriedler, and Hall struck him over the head with the butt of the gun. The strike was so hard that the handle of the gun broke, but it did not knock Kriedler unconscious. However, Kriedler died days later as a result of his wound.

The robbery was bold. A customer seated at the fountain counter in the store said, "The first bandit entered and commanded everyone into the backroom of the store." There they reportedly took the clerk's pocketbook, containing about four dollars; his watch; twenty-two dollars from the store's cash drawer; and a fountain pen. Another customer who interrupted the robbery was also robbed of his cash. "Mr. Kriedler drew his gun and pointed it at the bandits," the *South Bend Tribune* relayed. "He pulled the trigger two or three times but the gun failed to fire and the bandits grappled with him and struck him with his own gun. They then picked up the gun which [Kriedler] had dropped and fled."[57]

A series of other drug and grocery store robberies in South Bend, Mishawaka and Elkhart eventually led police to O'Brien and Hall as they attempted to burglarize an Elkhart business. After arresting the men, they also detained one of their female companions, Helen Young, twenty-two, of Mishawaka, after they found the broken gun connected to the Kriedler murder hidden in her sewing basket.

After his escape, O'Brien was eventually captured after making the mistake of getting drunk and approaching a plain-clothes Chicago police officer to ask for a dime so he could buy something to eat. The officer reported that he was dubious of O'Brien's claims of being destitute because he was well dressed at the time, although intoxicated. The officer said he'd give O'Brien a ride to a café but instead took him to a Chicago police substation. After he was fingerprinted and questioned, it was determined that O'Brien was a fugitive from the Elkhart County Jail.

"Since his escape…O'Brien has led authorities in Indiana on a merry chase," the *South Bend Tribune* reported. Police, expressing surprise that O'Brien had not tried to get farther away from South Bend then Chicago, had been the center of elaborate stories "of his comings and goings following his escape from the Goshen jail by sawing his way to freedom [and] soon became legion, constituting in local criminal annals a legend fast approaching in bulk such tales as might be told of a modern Robin Hood," the *South Bend Tribune* elaborately described.[58]

The *Tribune* continued, "But under all the stories of O'Brien, the facts remained. A law-abiding citizen was dead, struck down by lawlessness. The law enforcing machine, with ramifications in every city and hamlet in the nation, was seemingly impotent when it came to coping with the fugitive himself." While O'Brien enjoyed his freedom, his partner, Hall, stood trial in Elkhart County and, on September 27, 1926, after a two-week trial, was found guilty "by a jury of Goshen farmers and businessmen" who also recommended he be put to death. As his sentence was read, Hall took a cigar into his mouth and smiled broadly, gaining the title of the "laughing killer."[59]

South Bend police were now openly questioning whether the jail at Goshen was adequate to hold O'Brien, but attempts to transfer him to the state prison while he awaited trial were unsuccessful. Eventually, St. Joseph County authorities prevailed, and O'Brien was transferred to the county jail in South Bend, and his trial was moved to a court there. Elkhart County prosecutors who led the conviction of Hall were signed up to help their adjacent county cohorts. Transported to South Bend under heavy guard and chained at both his hands and feet, "a large audience waited near the county jail [in South Bend] for an hour before the Elkhart County officers came with O'Brien. O'Brien held his head down and protected his face with his arm when cameramen attempted to take pictures."[60]

O'Brien's trial finally got underway in early May 1927, and he was found guilty on a charge of murder but was sentenced to life in prison, eluding the death sentence that was given his partner, Hall. "O'Brien's face beamed when the verdict was read," newspaper reporters noted.

Hall's attorneys, who had won a temporary stay of his execution, said they would use the lighter sentence for O'Brien to buttress their efforts to keep their client from the electric chair. Their attempts, however, were unsuccessful, and Hall, now twenty-three years old, was electrocuted at the state prison in Michigan City on April 10, 1928.[61]

DESPERATE MEN, DESPERATE ACTS

Fugitive(s): Samuel Baxter and John Burns
Wanted For: February 7, 1928, escape, Tippecanoe County Jail, Lafayette, Indiana
February 7, 1928, murder of two police officers, Fowler, Indiana
Captured: Burns, May 21, 1928, Lafayette, Indiana
Baxter, August 27, 1931, Albuquerque, New Mexico

Just before Christmas 1927, the *Lafayette Journal & Courier* carried a small article near the bottom of page one about the arrest of three young men for the alleged holdup of a restaurant in West Point (a tiny Tippecanoe County settlement southwest of Lafayette).

Police alleged that Earl Middleton, twenty; Samuel Baxter, nineteen; and John Burns, twenty, robbed the cafe on December 13, 1927. Police said that, while under questioning, Middleton admitted his part in the holdup, though Baxter and Burns did not. Middleton eventually pleaded guilty to a robbery charge, while Baxter and Burns demanded a jury trial.[62]

"All three of the accused youths have been employed [in Lafayette] as taxi drivers," the *Journal & Courier* reported. "On the night of the robbery, it is alleged they borrowed an automobile from another man, drove to West Point, walked into the restaurant, played the piano and then without warning drew guns and took $75 from the restaurant proprietor, escaping in the automobile."[63]

During an initial trial in early January 1928, jurors deliberated for eighteen hours before announcing they were deadlocked on a verdict against Baxter and Burns. Complicating the case was the fact that Middleton had readily identified the two men as his accomplices while seeking his plea deal but at trial grew scared and refused to implicate Baxter and Burns.[64]

A second trial in the first week of February 1928 resulted in a guilty verdict against Baxter and Burns and a sentence of five to twenty-one years in the Indiana reformatory. Although they were under twenty-one at the time of the robbery, because both had prior criminal records, the judge was able to enhance their sentence.[65]

All that remained now was the transport of Baxter and Burns to the reformatory at Pendleton, about eighty miles southeast of Lafayette. The Tuesday morning, February 7, transport was routine business for two Tippecanoe County sheriff's deputies, John P. Grove, fifty-seven, and Wallace "Bill" McClure, fifty-five.

The deputies left the Tippecanoe County Jail just after 6:00 a.m. with their two prisoners in Grove's Studebaker touring car. "It was understood the two convicts were handcuffed together in the rear seat, McClure riding beside the driver [Grove] on the front seat," the *Lafayette Journal & Courier* reported. However, "From the moment they drove away from the jail, no trace of them has been reported."[66]

The deputies were expected back at the jail by noon, but when 3:00 p.m. arrived and they still were not back, concern began to grow. The shocking news that the deputies and their prisoners were missing quickly spread. The local American Legion and other fraternal organizations formed a citizen posse to assist in finding the men. Sheriff C.M. Johnston, confined to his home by illness, confirmed that Grove was driving to the Pendleton Reformatory for the first time, but McClure had transported many prisoners there before.[67]

The sheriff told reporters that it was not likely the young men had suddenly turned into murderers, but "it is believed they were desperate and overpowered the deputies and kidnapped them, and maybe tied them to a tree in some woods or some other out of the way spot." A day later, there was still no sign of the deputies and their charges or word about their whereabouts. The *Journal & Courier* reported, "The officers and their prisoners have vanished as complete as though wiped off of the earth by a hand from the sky."[68]

A.F. Miles, superintendent of the Pendleton Reformatory, joined the parade of officials with an opinion about what had happened. "It looks like foul play to me," he said. "It is a question with me what has happened. My impression is that the prisoners overpowered the officers and have gotten away with the automobile."[69]

The first clue was finally unearthed on February 9, 1928, when Burns's uncle Otto Smith who lived near Danville, Illinois, reported to authorities that his nephew and Baxter visited his home briefly that day—driving a Studebaker. Smith told police that he did not know the boys were fugitives at the time but learned of it later when he read a newspaper account. Smith insisted that Burns and Baxter were alone when they visited his rural home.[70]

On February 11, 1928, Decatur, Illinois police reported they had located Grove's Studebaker parked at a garage. The garage owner said it was brought to his shop by two young men, but they never returned for it. A search of the car revealed no blood stains, although a bullet hole in the windshield was noted.[71]

Hope for the fate of the deputies was broken nine days after they went missing, when the bodies of both Deputy Grove and McClure were found lying in a farm pasture near Fowler in Warren County (about fifty-five miles southwest of Lafayette and near the Indiana-Illinois state line). "Evidently the deputies had been placed there by Burns and Baxter, after the young convicts, now fugitives, had murdered the deputies and fled toward Illinois in Grove's car," the *Journal & Courier* recounted. "The scene of the gruesome discovery is but a short distance from the Illinois line, and the discovery came about through a visit which a land owner and two companions paid to the farm to estimate fence repairs."[72]

Police reported, "Although the corpses were in plain view of a north and south gravel road, nobody had seen them until a farmer and fence dealers stumbled upon them beside two trees at the edge of a small grove in a pasture lot east of the highway. The bodies were lying on the automobile robe that was missing from the bullet-marked Grove car when it was found in Decatur, Illinois....Evidently the two victims had been dragged or carried from the automobile into the field and laid carefully on the robe, one end of which had been thrown over Grove's face."[73]

On the day that private funeral services were announced for both deputies, the *Lafayette Journal & Courier* ran a large three-column photo of the men's bodies as they were found. An autopsy showed both men were shot from behind and were apparently shot with a gun other than the ones carried by Grove and McClure. "It's likely Burns and Baxter had weapons concealed on their person when they started from the county jail."[74] Grove was shot twice in his upper left shoulder, while McClure was shot once in the back and four other times in his arm. McClure's head was also crushed, "indicating that he had been struck from the rear with some heavy instrument."[75]

Burns and Baxter remained elusive fugitives, but at least a partial sigh of relief was offered on May 21, 1928—some three months after the shocking murders—when local, state and federal authorities conducted an early morning raid at a home at 204 West Thornell Street in West Lafayette and found Burns hiding there. The home, owned by Burns's uncle and aunt, Mr. and Mrs. George Williamson, had been under surveillance after a tip was received. The Williamsons had raised Burns from the time he was a young boy.

"It is an established tradition in connection with crime that the criminal will eventually return to the scene of his deed," the editors of the *Lafayette Journal & Courier* declared. "Burns finally succumbed to a desire to visit his home, a decision that cost him his liberty. When the authorities visited the Williamson home, they proceeded to search the house and found the much-wanted young man hiding beneath a rug behind a davenport. Although his appearance has changed so materially as to make him almost unrecognizable, he made no attempt to deny his identity."[76]

Questioned for almost twelve hours, Burns offered an inconsistent story about what had happened. He spun a tale that two other unknown men had intercepted their car en route to the reformatory and were responsible for killing the deputies. Burns told authorities that he and Baxter left Decatur, Illinois, by jumping a freight train and ended up in East St. Louis, Missouri, and then jumped another train and made it as far as Kansas City and eventually Oklahoma. He said he and Baxter were arrested on minor charges at Atoka, Oklahoma, and held for thirty-six days, but authorities there failed to make the connection between them and the Indiana murders.

His elaborate tale included accounts of getting a job in Tennessee and returning to his aunt's home just a day before he was arrested.

"When Baxter and I were arrested at Atoka, Oklahoma, I felt they had the goods on us, that they knew we were the ones wanted and just gave us the 36 days to hold us until the officers came from Lafayette.…Those 36 days seemed like 36 years." After they were released, Burns and Baxter decided to separate from each other. "We decided that traveling together, we would be more apt to be recognized. I wanted to come back to Lafayette many times, and stayed away just as long as I could," Burns told a reporter. "There are people there who have done a lot for me and of whom I think a great deal. It just goes to show, though, that you can't be smarter than the law. I thought I could slip in, see those I wanted to see, and slip out tonight."[77]

On June 8, 1928, Burns was found guilty on two counts of murder following a four-day trial. Tippecanoe County judge Homer W. Hennegar sentenced him to life in prison. As one local newspaper account told, "The sentencing of the youth, whose career has been marked by almost constant rebellion against the laws that protect society from criminals, takes him away forever from a wild life that has found him repeatedly in trouble."[78]

While the Burns half of the case was resolved, Baxter remained elusive and a highly wanted fugitive from Indiana until August 27, 1931, when police in Albuquerque, New Mexico, announced they had arrested Baxter. He had been free for three and a half years.

He was shot in the leg by police as he attempted to flee, and the *Albuquerque Journal* reported that Baxter was "lying on a cot in St. Joseph's Hospital with a bullet wound in his right leg, a man positively identified by fingerprints.… He steadfastly refused to talk to officers."[79]

Working under the name of Al Casey, Baxter was employed as a steel construction foreman on a water tower under construction at the Veterans Bureau building in Albuquerque. While he was on the run, Baxter had taken a wife and was now the father of a seven-month-old child and rented a home in the city. His wife and child visited him briefly at the hospital, and his wife reportedly had no knowledge of his criminal past in Indiana.

Baxter continued to deny his true identity, but ultimately failed in efforts to fight extradition to Indiana. On September 1, 1931, the Tippecanoe County sheriff arrived in Albuquerque to help escort Baxter by ambulance to a local train. Once on the train, he was to be handcuffed to his hospital bed for the remainder of the trip (still recovering from his severe leg wound).

"Baxter's only words on the journey from the hospital to the train were of thanks to one jailor and the ambulance men for their careful handling of his leg," the *Albuquerque Journal* reported. "He left here his young wife and their baby who are expected to go to the woman's former home in McGregor, Texas. The wife (twenty-year-old Minnie Yeager) still believes the man to be Al Casey. She was not at the station."[80] Forty-eight hours later, Baxter arrived at the train station in Lafayette to a large crowd of onlookers. He was lifted from the train still on a cot, unable to walk.

By the end of September, Baxter's new bride and son had relocated to Lafayette and were staying with his parents, who continued to proclaim their son's innocence. In early October came news that the lower portion of Baxter's leg had to be removed, as the gunshot wound he received while being arrested was so damaging. After his amputation, he was placed in the Tippecanoe County Jail to await trial for the murders of the sheriff's deputies.[81]

The murder trial got underway in the first week of January 1932, and Baxter admitted that he had struck McClure with a blunt object in an attempt to escape but denied having shot Deputy McClure and Grove to death. He accused his partner in crime, John Burns, of shooting the men. Jurors were unconvinced and convicted Baxter of second-degree murder. He was sentenced to life in prison on January 9, 1932.

"The verdict of the jury returned at 11:27 o'clock Friday night was a great shock to the defendant and his family and friends who were expecting a milder penalty," the *Lafayette Journal & Courier* reported. "Baxter's reformation after his escape from the scene of the crime, his wife and baby, and his record as a workman, had won him friends and the fact that he had been crippled for life as a result of an infection setting in after he had been shot and wounded also aroused sympathy."[82]

2

1930-39

A COP TURNED KILLER ROBS THE LOTTERY

Fugitive(s): William C. Hill, Harold Lester, James Trout and James Leach
Wanted For: March 12, 1930, robbery and murder, Indianapolis, Indiana
Captured: Hill and Lester, March 24, 1930, Indianapolis, Indiana
Trout and Leach, April 3, 1930, Orlando, Florida

At the beginning of the 1930s, Orlando was little more than a small dot on the state map of Florida. The Orange County community boasted fewer than fifty thousand residents. The Florida land boom of the 1920s was over, and the Depression was at hand, and a once-promising tourism business had all but dried up. At the time, four decades before Walt Disney invaded the region, Orlando made sense as a comfortable and out-of-the-way place for some Indiana fugitives to hide.

The two Hoosiers wanted for murder, James Trout (also known as Lee Gootee), twenty-three, and his companion, James Leach, twenty-two, fled to Orlando, one thousand miles south of Indianapolis and far from the manhunt underway for them.

It all came to an end on April 3, 1930, as Trout and Leach were stopped in a stolen sedan with Indiana license plates on an Orlando street. They told police they were from Hammond, Indiana, and attempted to produce paperwork to prove they owned the car.[83] Fingerprints, photographs and telegrams between police in Orlando and Indianapolis confirmed, however, that the men were both wanted—Trout for murder and Leach for "auto banditry" and for theft for "blowing the safe" of an Indianapolis auto dealer.[84]

The murder, for which Trout was sought, was one that had made big headlines in Indianapolis less than a month earlier. The murder victim, Charles Zeller, fifty-one, of Indianapolis, had big dreams of being an important man. With the help of an organized group of associates, Zeller had worked the many meat butcher and packing companies across the near south side of the city to become "king" of a popular lottery for working men.

The Butchers and Packers' Lottery, as it was known, gave hardworking men a chance to win prizes that, in 1930s dollars, represented big money—as much as $1,000 at a time. On Wednesday evening, March 12, 1930, however, Zeller's growing empire came to an end on the sidewalk outside his humble wood frame home at 320 East Southern Avenue in a working-class Garfield Park neighborhood.

On that evening, a gunman jumped from a car parked behind Zeller, and one of his top lieutenants, Don C. Cutshaw, forty-two, opened fire. After dropping Zeller with the bullets, the bandits seized the suitcase Zeller famously carried with him everywhere. Zeller had exited the car to speak to an approaching neighbor, identified as Frank Gardina, when shots rang out.

"Two men with dark handkerchiefs pulled up over their chins and automatics in their hands slipped out of the parked car behind Cutshaw's automobile," the *Indianapolis Star* reported. Witnesses said Zeller raised his hands at the demand made of him: "Give me that gun and bag!" Zeller reportedly refused to comply and was shot, falling to the sidewalk, and then shot twice more while lying prostrate on the cold ground.[85]

Police said Zeller was alive and talking when they arrived on the scene, and he insisted that he had been the victim of "an ordinary robbery" at the hands of a trigger-happy assailant. Police later seized a magazine from a .38-caliber automatic pistol that landed on Zeller's front lawn. A stolen car believed to be driven by the men involved in the shooting was later recovered on the city's east side.

Police were not buying Zeller's story—he was a known entity to them—and they understood from the start that the robbery and shooting were directly related to the illegal lottery he operated. Police not only held but also arrested Zeller's unwounded associate, Cutshaw, on a charge of vagrancy related to his activity with the lottery.

"Cutshaw said that normally on Wednesday night both men carried large sums of money, but that last night Zeller had only $50," the *Star* reported.[86]

Other than that, Cutshaw was not cooperating, refusing to provide details on the lottery and its customers or even where the weekly lottery draws were conducted. "The theory expressed by police is that the gunmen believed that Zeller had $1,500 or more in a bag he carried, which was to be distributed in lottery prizes," the *Star* noted.[87]

The robbery case turned into a murder case when Zeller expired at City Hospital on Saturday, March 15, 1930.[88]

The story took an amazing turn ten days later, when newspapers across the state declared the startling news that Indianapolis police had arrested one of their own former officers, twenty-five-year-old William C. Hill, dismissed from the force just three months earlier, for the Zeller murder. Beneath a photo of the uniformed Hill, the *Indianapolis Star* explained that Hill had gone from hero to felon in less than two years.

"From the obscurity of a 'greenhorn,' but with several months of experience behind him," the *Star* reported, "a modest, unassuming young patrolman found himself overnight the hero of the Indianapolis Police Department. That was in September 1928 when singled-handed, a young Hill captured two automobile thieves in a revolver battle and recovered two stolen cars and loot valued at $500." Fast-forward to March 24, 1930, and Hill, described by reporters as "plain" but "a big fellow," was "slated at the city prison on a charge of murder." Detectives said Hill confessed to shooting and fatally wounding Zeller in the robbery attempt two weeks earlier.[89]

"He smiled with a trace of bitterness when curious passers-by stared at him as he was being taken from police headquarters to the county jail across the street, reminded perhaps of the day [in 1928] when fellow officers and friends stared at him in admiration and when reporters sought to question him and photographers asked him to pose." The *Indianapolis Star* account told, "The 'big fellow's' shoulders did not have the same jaunty swing as they did a year and a half ago and he kept his eyes on the pavement ahead of him."[90]

In addition to Hill, police arrested Harold Lester, twenty-six, who was said to be an accomplice in planning the robbery. Lester provided information about the Butchers and Packers' Lottery and assisted police in unraveling the conspiracy to rob the illegal operation. Lester reportedly felt double crossed in the entire affair because he had helped plan the operation, but he insisted that Hill had left him out on the night of the actual raid on Zeller.

Detectives explained that they focused quickly on Hill and his associates, based on witness statements, and questioned him repeatedly for more than a week. "Hill steadfastly had denied his guilt, but finally broke down under severe questioning and confessed, detectives said, to the holdup and shooting," the *Star* reported.[91]

During his trial for the murder of Zeller, Hill made an unsuccessful escape attempt from the Marion County Courthouse. "I almost made it," Hill muttered as he was wrestled to the courthouse floor by a court bailiff and a courtroom witness. "I had nothing to lose," Hill said.[92]

"While the attention of attorneys and spectators in the court chamber was centered on principals in a minor case before the judge, Hill hurdled the front railing of the jury box, sprawled under an iron railing that separates the judge's compartment from spectators, raced down the aisle to the rear door and into the second floor corridor of the Courthouse," the *Indianapolis Star* reported.[93]

Hill might have succeeded in his escape, except for a court spectator identified as Mort O'Hare, a former football tackle, and John G. Willis, a court employee. Both men tackled Hill in the courthouse hallway and returned him to custody.

In January 1931, Hill reversed his plea and entered a plea of guilty on a charge of first-degree murder in Hamilton County Circuit Court in Noblesville, where his case was moved on a change of venue from Indianapolis. He was sentenced to life in prison at the Indiana State Prison in Michigan City. Hill wept as he was escorted from the courtroom in shackles.[94]

It was a sad ending for an officer who had told reporters in 1928, after his successful arrest of auto thieves resulted in some high profile arrests, "You see, I expect to be a policeman the rest of my life and I'm taking this job seriously."[95]

"WEE WILLIE" MASON—MADE FOR THE HEADLINES

Fugitive(s): "Wee Willie" Mason
Wanted For: February 7, 1933, murder and robbery, Indianapolis, Indiana
August 21, 1934, escape, Hamilton County Jail, Noblesville, Indiana
Captured: March 20, 1933, Erlander, Kentucky
November 10, 1934, Carrollton, Kentucky

News reporters seemingly couldn't get enough of the exploits of "Wee Willie" Mason, a bespectacled Indianapolis criminal who eventually gave up his left foot, and his life, in furtherance of forays into crime.

The crime for which Mason gained the most fame was the tragic slaying of Indianapolis police sergeant Lester Jones during the early morning robbery of an Indianapolis interurban bus barn on February 7, 1933. Mason was apparently the brains behind the idea to raid the safe and cash drawers of the Peoples Motor Coach Company at Twenty-Second and Yandes Streets on the city's Near Northside. Jones and fellow officers were dispatched to the bus company on a complaint of "trouble," with few other details. Because the initial report to police did not indicate that an armed robbery led by eight gunmen was underway, Jones and other officers approached casually without their weapons drawn.

They found bus passengers and Luther Standard, described in an *Indianapolis News* account as "a colored service man," being "terrorized by a gang of desperadoes." Standard, who witnessed the initial deadly assault on Jones and other officers was able to crawl undetected to a back office and called police a second time and let them know of the gun battle underway. "Send all the police you got, all hell's broken loose," Standard whispered to the police dispatcher.[96]

Jones and his men arrived just as the bandits were attempting their getaway, but they were struggling to get the car out of the bus garage they had commandeered during the robbery. One of the gunmen, holding a machine gun, warned the others of the approaching cops. Standard said, "When Sergeant Jones walked in, they let him have it. He didn't have a chance. Then they all came out and one guy said, 'scram' and they did, but they couldn't get out. They didn't know how many police were there." The *Indianapolis News* account breathlessly relayed that after he was shot, Jones "managed to raise himself and attempted to draw his weapon. Loss of blood, however, prevented this, and, mortally wounded, he dragged himself across the street, where he died before medical aid reached him."[97]

Other officers braved "a shower of machine gun fire and stood over Jones' fallen body and exchanged gunfire with the bandits, who continued to fire recklessly." The other officers present were identified as Patrolmen Michael McAllen and Willard Hawkins.[98]

McAllen told reporters, "We got a report by radio that there was a fuss at the coach company's barn. Sergeant Jones remarked we might as well hurry up there and see what was going on. We did not have any idea of what we were running into. In fact, we figured it was just a fight and that it would soon be over." He said Jones approached the bus garage door "and rolled it back, and all hell broke loose. Poor Lester, the first burst of machine gun fire got him. He was sprayed with bullets. He just sort of wilted and fell to the ground. I grabbed my gun and started to shoot. There wasn't anything else I could do. It was my neck or someone else's."[99]

With Sergeant Jones felled and the getaway car still lodged behind garage doors, the eight robbers fled on foot, leaving behind several of their weapons and two bags that contained their stolen loot and a bullet ridden bus station. The investigation later showed one bag contained $1,869 from the office safe and $323 from cash drawers.[100]

Once the dust settled, Standard told reporters that the scene was "just like a movie I saw the night before last. Only worse. We thought when the car drove in and the fellows shut the steel doors again that they were some sort of night force. Then when they jumped out with their guns and one of them grabbed the one-armed night watchman, stuck a gun in his ribs and said, 'Shut up and keep shut up,' we knew there was trouble."[101]

Standard said he left a bus tire mechanic, M.H. Lewis, to watch the men while he snuck away to make the original "trouble" call to the police. "I slipped into one of the back offices, turned off the lights, crawled along the floor, back of a desk and phoned," Standard said. "The second time I slipped into an office further back the same way." Among the weapons in use by the bandit was a machine gun. "They had the machine gun right out there in front I guess, for when the squad car came up, the man who held it ran in and said, 'Here they come!' One man rushed out with the bag of money and threw it in the car, but they couldn't get the car out, for the doors were shut."[102]

A massive statewide manhunt was undertaken, and Indiana authorities notified those in neighboring states, and with the help of radio station reports, news of the fugitives spread quickly.

Jones was a well-known and popular officer, the former head of the department's traffic division. His wife, the newly widowed Goldie Mildred Jones, said, "He had always hoped he would go out that way, he was not afraid of anything." He was a native of Indianapolis and serving on the police force had been a lifelong dream for Jones. Mayor Reginald H. Sullivan noted, "Sergeant Jones was a brave man and a fine man and Patrolmen McAllen and Hawkins are brave men also. I take my hat off to them and to the entire Indianapolis Police Department."[103]

Eventually, police at Erlanger, Kentucky, rounded up five of the eight bandits in the Indianapolis heist on March 20, following a series of robberies in that state, and the final three were apprehended on April 23 in Louisville. In addition to Mason, thirty, the bandits captured were identified as Arthur Nichols, thirty-nine; Edwin P. Miller, thirty-six; Richard Keller, twenty-seven; Eddie "Foggy" Dean, thirty-two; Ernest G. Thompson, thirty-two; George Murphy, thirty-five; and Fred Adams, thirty-seven. When seized by police, the men were found to be in possession of a large stash of guns, including a machine gun, sticks of dynamite, dynamite caps, fuses, two short-wave radio sets and piles of ammunition.[104]

During the house raid at Erlander, Kentucky, Mason was found asleep in a bed with a bullet wound to his left foot. Murphy was also healing from another bullet wound to his ankle. It was unclear if the men had been shot in the Indianapolis gun battle more than a month earlier or in a subsequent robbery. Mason's wound was so badly infected that his foot was amputated.

"Quite a procession started for Indianapolis," *Indianapolis Star* reporter Mary E. Bostwick wrote. "There was Mason in a City Hospital ambulance, and four automobiles, including the one in which the bandits escaped and had stolen from [Indianapolis]….There was a large number of police in the convoy, all heavily armed. The prisoners were arraigned in criminal court in Indianapolis, and Mason was brought in on a stretcher."[105]

"Hobbling on crutches necessitated by the amputation of his left foot, Mason joked and talked with policemen" as he was fingerprinted and photographed.[106] In the weeks that followed, several of Mason's cohorts took plea agreements for prison sentences. Mason and co-defendant "Foggy" Dean won a change of venue motion and had their case transferred to adjacent Hamilton County. Both men were tried at Noblesville in November 1933, for two weeks, but two juries called to hear the cases, failed to reach a verdict and were dismissed as a mistrial was declared.

As Mason and Dean awaited a second trial on August 21, 1934, headlines screamed the news that hacksaws smuggled into the aging Hamilton County Jail had succeeded in allowing Mason and four others to escape. Dean was not among those who fled the seventy-five-year-old jail. "The daring jail break, led by Mason who was facing a second trial for the cold-blooded murder of an Indianapolis police officer, was discovered when Sheriff Frank Hattery failed to hear the customary snoring of the prisoners in their cells," the Associated Press reported.[107]

Indianapolis authorities prevailed on Hamilton County authorities to transfer Dean back to the more secure and modern Marion County Jail. Being in a new, larger jail didn't mean attempts to break free were eliminated. In September 1934, deputies intercepted a jar of strawberry preserves dropped off at the jail by a young boy for a fugitive held for New York City authorities. Dean was implicated in the plot that consisted of dynamite blasting caps hidden in the strawberry preserves, which were planned to blow cell blocks.[108]

Another member of Mason's gang, Ernest Thompson, had also staged a getaway, walking out of the Hamilton County Jail in February 1934 by blending in with a group of CWA workers hired by the county to make upgrades to the jail. "He was reported hither and yon, and was said to be frequenting Indianapolis," media reports indicated.[109]

In November 1934, Mason was recaptured by police at Carrollton, Kentucky. He was reported unarmed and did not resist and was again returned to Indianapolis to face a second trial for the murder of Sergeant Jones.[110] Dean was also later recaptured, and both men were convicted in 1935 for the policeman's murder.

In June 1953, the Indiana Parole Board voted to release both Mason and Dean after both men had served eighteen-year sentences at the Indiana State Prison. Before the parole board, Mason repeated claims he made at trial that he did not know who had actually shot Sergeant Jones. While behind bars, Mason had become known as the "dean of the prison gangs" at Michigan City, but he still convinced parole board members that now that he was fifty-three years old, he planned to follow the straight and narrow path.[111]

THE DARING DILLINGER GANG

Fugitive(s): John Dillinger, John "Red" Hamilton, Homer Van Meter, Charles Makley, Russell Lee Clark, Tommy Carroll, Harold "Eddie" Green, Harry "Pete" Pierpont, Harry E. Copeland and Edward Shouse

Wanted For: September 26, 1933, escape, Indiana State Prison, Michigan City, Indiana

October 12, 1933, escape and murder, Allen County Jail, Lima, Ohio

October 14, 1933, police station robbery, Auburn, Indiana

October 23, 1933, bank robbery, Greencastle, Indiana

January 15, 1934, bank robbery and murder, East Chicago, Indiana

March 3, 1934, escape, Lake County Jail, Crown Point, Indiana

April 12, 1934, police station robbery, Warsaw, Indiana

June 30, 1934, bank robbery and murder, South Bend, Indiana

Death: Green, April 10, 1934, St. Paul, Minnesota
Hamilton, April 26, 1934, Aurora, Illinois
Carroll, June 7, 1934, Waterloo, Iowa
Dillinger, July 22, 1934, Chicago, Illinois
Van Meter, August 23, 1934, St. Paul, Minnesota
Makley, September 22, 1934, Columbus, Ohio
Pierpont, October 17, 1934, Columbus, Ohio
Shouse, September 14, 1959, Terre Haute, Indiana
Copeland, December 7, 1963, Livonia, Michigan
Clark, December 24, 1968, Detroit, Michigan

No consideration of Indiana fugitives would be complete without a review of the most famous fugitive the state ever produced, John Herbert Dillinger, elevated to prominence as the FBI's first Public Enemy No. 1 in 1933–34.

Although gang affiliations could be loosely made, and changed, a determined and deadly group of ten men (half of them fellow Hoosiers) joined Dillinger in an amazing spree of crime covering a two-year period in 1933 and 1934. Decades later, books, films and television shows continue to explore the exploits of the Dillinger gang, which found its genesis behind the bars of the Indiana State Prison in Michigan City.

Dillinger was a fugitive on more than one occasion but only once from Indiana authorities after breaking out of the so-called escape-proof Lake County Jail at Crown Point on March 3, 1934. His first escape came in October 1933, following his arrest in Ohio for the robbery of a bank in Lima.

Born in Indianapolis in 1903, Dillinger lived his childhood trapped in poverty without his mother, who died when he was a toddler, and soon found trouble. In 1916, when Dillinger was thirteen years old, his father moved the family to a rural Morgan County farm (near Mooresville) in one last attempt to save John from a life of crime. His father's efforts notwithstanding, Dillinger was arrested for auto theft in 1922 and later dishonorably discharged from the U.S. Navy. Dillinger ran seriously afoul of the law when he was twenty-one years old, in 1924, for beating and robbing a local grocery store owner. A Morgan County judge showed no mercy, handing young Dillinger two separate sentences for robbery and felony conspiracy and another for assault and battery with intent to rob.

In May 1933, the State Clemency Commission finally considered Dillinger for release from the brutal Michigan City prison, but by then, he had formed deep relationships with several accomplished criminals. Chief among them was Harry "Pete" Pierpont, a seasoned criminal from Muncie with a string of bank robberies dating to the 1920s under his belt.[112]

Released on May 10, 1933, Dillinger returned to his father's home with few prospects for employment. Not only was the Great Depression and a drought devastating Indiana (and most of the nation), a man with a criminal record in small-town Indiana in the 1930s could forget about any grace or forgiveness from the locals.

Police believe Dillinger turned to crime just over a month after getting out of jail, suspected of robbing the New Carlisle National Bank in St. Joseph County on June 21, 1933. The take, a reported $10,000, likely whetted his appetite for more, and the Dillinger gang was in full force. Dillinger was also a suspect that spring in a string of bank robberies at Daleville, Montpelier and Bluffton. In August 1933, Dillinger turned his sights on a bigger bank in Indianapolis, a robbery that netted him $24,800.

His luck ran out in September 1933, when he was nabbed near Dayton, Ohio, for the robbery of an Ohio bank. Jailed at the Allen County Jail in Lima, Dillinger gang members (several of whom had busted out of the Indiana State Prison on September 26, 1933) were determined to free their leader.

That determination had already proven deadly on December 20, 1933. Shouse and two female companions engaged in a gun battle with police officers from Indiana and Illinois who attempted to corner several of them where they were hiding in tiny Paris, Illinois (twenty-two miles northwest of Terre Haute). Indiana State Police trooper Eugene Teague was killed in the battle (later determined to have been shot by a fellow officer in the confusion of the shoot-out). Shouse was captured but not before another police officer was killed.[113]

Captain Matt Leach, who had to console fellow officers who had accidentally killed one of their own, explained, "It was an unfortunate, unavoidable occurrence. Nobody can be blamed for the accident."[114]

With Dillinger still housed at the Allen County Jail in Lima, gang members led by Pierpont descended on the town on Friday the thirteenth of October 1933. Once at the jail, they attempted to convince the sheriff that they were federal agents sent to retrieve Dillinger. Unconvinced, Sheriff Jess L. Sarber refused to release Dillinger and was shot and killed. It was the first but not the last time Dillinger would be linked to a murder. The trigger man in Sheriff Sarber's death was identified as Pierpont.

"Another entry in the sensational crime record of John Dillinger, paroled convict, was being made Friday as state and local police opened a statewide search for the desperado following his liberation from jail at Lima, Ohio, and the slaying of Jess Sarber, sheriff," the *Indianapolis Star* reported.[115]

Dillinger's group of men included five fellow Hoosiers, Pierpont, Russell Lee Clark of Terre Haute, Harry E. Copeland of Muncie, Edward Shouse of Milford (Decatur County) and Homer Van Meter of Fort Wayne. "New" friends acquired through his prison stint included John "Red" Hamilton (a Canadian native); Charles Makley of St. Mary's, Ohio; Tommy Carroll of Red Lodge, Montana; Harold "Eddie" Green of Pueblo, Colorado; and even "Baby Face Nelson," also known as Lester J. Gillis of Chicago.

With the exception of Makley (born fourteen years before Dillinger), all of the men recruited for the Dillinger gang were, just like him, born at the start of the twentieth century and rising into adulthood with few options for success, seemingly locked into poverty and want. Dillinger and his gang became romanticized folk heroes of their era. Robbing at least twelve banks (many of the same ones that had foreclosed home and farm mortgages held by many working families) and taking an estimated $400,000 in cash in a two-year period, Dillinger also reportedly stole and destroyed bank mortgage paperwork as a sign of good faith.[116]

After the Ohio jail break, the Dillinger gang kicked into high gear in the just over six months that followed, first robbing the Auburn Police Department on October 14, 1933, for guns and ammunition. Days later, the Central National Bank at Greencastle was robbed of $16,000 in cash and $60,000 in bonds.[117]

Most members of the gang hid out in the intervening months, until a January 15, 1934 robbery and shootout at the First National Bank of East Chicago, leaving Patrick O'Malley, an East Chicago policeman, dead. The robbery reportedly netted Dillinger another $20,000, but for the second time, he was tied to the murder of a law enforcement officer.

Reporters at the *Hammond Times* seem conflicted—excited that East Chicago was the center of the action and mournful of O'Malley's death: "East Chicago is just settling down this morning after its biggest thrill in years occasioned by the daring raid of two bandits on the First National Bank.…The tragic murder of Police Officer Patrick O'Malley is universally mourned by citizens and members of the department."[118]

Eventually, Dillinger, Clark, Bakley and Pierpont were captured in "a bloodless coup" on January 26, 1934, in Tucson, Arizona. Police there were tipped off by a local who saw a picture of Dillinger on a wanted poster and took the quartet without incident.

An International News Service correspondent quoted Dillinger as complaining, "Somebody has dealt me a rotten hand. We had come to Arizona to quit the game and rest. We were through. None of us liked [bank robbing] anyway. We thought no one would know us way out here. Why, this is the end of the world. Just look at this dreary desert, if you don't believe it. Some of my friends told me that we might run into trouble, but Tucson is so far away from thickly populated places that I didn't think there was a chance."[119]

Returned to Indiana to face murder and robbery charges for the East Chicago job, Dillinger's presence in the state was a media circus. Regrettably, Lake County prosecutor Robert G. Estill and Sheriff Lillian M. Holley posed for casual pictures with Dillinger when he arrived at the jail in Crown Point. Their casual approach to Dillinger would come back to haunt them, as members of the Dillinger gang sprang him from the county lockup on March 3, 1934, with Dillinger using a fake gun made of soap (darkened with shoe polish) to accomplish his freedom.

Despite his earlier assertions that he and his gang were tired of robbing banks and running from the police, they returned to their regular habits quickly. In need of weapons to resume their activities, they robbed the Warsaw Police Department on April 12, 1934, taking weapons and ammunition.

While police ran down reports that Dillinger had moved in and out of Morgan County freely on visits to his family, he remained at large until the gang struck again. On June 30, 1934, the gang pulled one more job on a busy Saturday morning at the Merchants National Bank in downtown South Bend. Things did not go well as a shootout ensued after the bank alarm was sounded, and city patrolman Howard Wagner was killed, and four others were injured. The gang still made off with nearly $30,000.[120]

With three Indiana police officers now dead, it is not surprising that federal authorities showed Dillinger no mercy when they surrounded him outside the Biograph Theatre in Chicago on a warm July 22, 1934, and riddled his body with bullets. His violent death mirrored that of other members of the gang, including Carroll, Green, Hamilton, Makley, Nelson and Van Meter, who all died in shootouts with police.

Pierpont was executed on October 17, 1934, by the State of Ohio for the murder of Sheriff Sarber. An Associated Press dispatch from the prison noted, Pierpont, "the fair-haired 'brains' of the dissolved Dillinger mob was electrocuted early today—the first of the nomadic gang of robbers and killers to receive by legal process the full wages of crime. Quietly, unaided and with the ghost of a smile on his lips, the thirty-two-year-old killer sat down to death in the gaunt wooden chair within the high stockade of a prison guarded in unprecedented fashion." Reporters seemed disappointed that there were no last words from Pierpoint. "He volunteered none," the AP noted. "He just sat down with a rueful smile, closed his eyes, strained the muscles of his lanky, six-foot-two frame as the current struck, clenched one fist, and that was all."[121]

Shouse, Copeland and Clark all finished out lengthy prison sentences and were eventually released. Their deaths, many decades later, were barely noted. Shouse died at the age of fifty-four in 1959, Copeland died at age sixty-seven in 1963 and Clark succumbed to cancer at age seventy in 1968.

HONEYMOON FUGITIVES

Fugitive(s): Robert York, Mary York and Robert Mobley
Wanted For: May 17, 1938, escape from Indiana Reformatory guards while attending mother's funeral, Indianapolis, Indiana
May–October 1938, robberies, Indiana and Missouri
Captured: October 30, 1938, Frankfort, Indiana

"Cell bars separated Robert York, elusive 19-year-old gunman, and his pretty young wife today at the end of a thrilling, crime-dotted honeymoon," the *Indianapolis News* reported. "York admitted to detectives that he had mixed romance and robbery in a criss-cross fugitive flight between two states—Indiana and Missouri."[122]

After becoming a fugitive from Indiana, York fled to Missouri and promptly tied the knot with seventeen-year-old Mary Griner of Eldon, Missouri, after a brief courtship. York was a fugitive from the Indiana Reformatory at the time he took his vows, but Mary would later tell detectives she was unaware of her new husband's tenuous status as a free man. Even so, it didn't matter— she was in love.

York's escape from prison custody had been a family affair as well. He slipped from the custody of guards while attending his mother's Indianapolis funeral on May 17, 1938. "As his guards stood with their heads bowed [in prayer] at the funeral of his mother, Mrs. Ada York, he slipped away," the *Indianapolis News* reported. York had been granted special permission to attend the funeral as an act of kindness by the warden of the prison. However, once at the funeral service at a Near Northside funeral home, "he slid out of his seat, dashed to the door and disappeared on a side street as the minister prayed," one newspaper account told.[123]

Before his funeral exodus, York had only been housed at the Indiana Reformatory for one year, sentenced at the age of eighteen to a ten-year term for auto theft. At the time of his sentencing, York told the judge, "You might as well give me life, judge. I can't get a decent job and every time I get out, the police are on my trail, hoping to catch me in something. Prisons make criminals instead of curing them of crime."[124]

In the weeks following his escape, Robert met Mary in Missouri, and it was true love. Married and eager to be on their own, the young couple made their way west to Iowa and engaged in a variety of holdups in numerous communities along the way. The new bride, Mary, implicated herself and her husband in several armed robberies and similarly named their friend Harold Mobley, twenty, as a conspirator in some of their heists.

Mary told detectives she had only known York for three weeks when she agreed to marry him and knew nothing of his prison past. Asked how she became acquainted with him, she replied, "Oh, he just came around."[125]

Their brief union suffered a major setback as York attempted to visit family members in Frankfort, Indiana, on a quiet Sunday, October 30, 1938. Tipped off that York would be in town for a visit, police nabbed Robert, Mary and their friend Mobley at a Frankfort rooming house. During the arrest, police recovered three revolvers carried by York, a blackjack, a hunting knife and three hundred shells.

The courts were not in awe of the young love that had resulted in a marital union between Robert and Mary. Robert was ordered returned to the Indiana Reformatory at Pendleton to complete the rest of his ten-year sentence, while Mary York and Mobley were returned to Franklin County, Missouri, to face numerous robbery charges.[126] Prosecutors later changed their mind and got Robert York to agree to waive extradition to face more charges in Missouri, helping authorities gain convictions against his two cohorts.[127]

Before returning to a jail cell for good, Robert York provided colorful quotes to newspaper reporters. He told one that he saved money from mowing lawns in his Indianapolis neighborhood to buy his first gun at the age of seventeen. He admitted to "pulling a small job" by randomly targeting an automobile driver in the city "before going for larger loot….I intended to be an artist, but I was attracted by thrills and deliberately planned to be a holdup man." And despite reports that he had engaged in more crimes after he escaped from his mother's funeral, he admitted that he considered "going straight" for a while but gave up on the idea.[128]

Following a November 1938 trial in Union, Missouri, Robert York was found guilty of armed robbery and sentenced to forty years in prison. His new bride, Mary, was acquitted. His accomplice, Mobley, was found guilty and given a three-year sentence.[129]

A MURDER, A MOTHER AND A FUGITIVE

Fugitive(s): Oliver Watters
Wanted For: June 25, 1938, kidnapping, South Bend, Indiana
Captured: May 10, 1939, New York City

On the day she tracked down her husband on a New York City street, despite having murdered her mother-in-law, Roberta Watters was not the fugitive. It was her estranged husband, Oliver, who was wanted.

On May 10, 1939, twenty-nine-year-old Roberta waved down a New York City police officer on Fourteenth Street and begged his help in arresting her husband, whom, after three years of searching, she had just found in his hiding place amid the sea of more than seven million people in the city.

"Come quick! There's my husband! I've been looking for him for three years for stealing my children!" Roberta screamed, and after taking him to a New York Police Department precinct house, the whole story was untangled. Oliver, thirty-five, working as an accountant and labor organizer, was held by Detective William A. Duffy for return to South Bend, Indiana.[130]

It was an ironic turn of events because while Oliver was wanted for the kidnapping of the couple's two children, Eugene, nine, and Gala, five, it was Roberta who had shot and killed Oliver's mother in her pursuit of the children. Amazingly cleared of the point-blank murder of her mother-in-law, Roberta spent the subsequent months working as a child's nurse and hitchhiked her way to New York City after learning Oliver was hiding there.

Rewind to a year earlier on April 28, 1938, and it was Roberta Watters, not Oliver, who was in police custody. On that day, as the *South Bend Tribune* reported, "The alert, dark eyes of Roberta Watters, clouded with emotion when she learned that she may face a first-degree murder charge for the fatal shooting of her mother-in-law." Dead was Martha E. Watters, sixty-three, who was shot two days earlier, as she refused to tell Roberta where her children were. Reporters and detectives observing Roberta's reaction that she had shot her mother-in-law to death noted that she quickly gained her composure, declaring, "It's going to complicate things, but it won't make any difference in my life. I couldn't go on the other way without the children."[131]

St. Joseph County officials moved quickly to charge Roberta with murder, setting aside any effort to help her find her two children, still held out of her reach somewhere by her estranged husband of six years. In a signed statement to police, Roberta said she had gone to Martha's home not with the intent of shooting her but desperately wanting to know where her children were.

"I wouldn't have taken anybody with me if I expected to do that," Roberta said, reminding reporters that she had told local authorities she was coming to South Bend in search of her children, and had been accompanied on the day of the shooting by deputy prosecutor Wilford V. Walz. As Martha told Walz that she did not know where the children were, Roberta "overheard the remarks, frustrated in her quest for her children, and cast away discretion, strode to the porch where Mr. Walz was conversing with the woman and demanded, 'Where are my children?!'" Heated words were passed back and forth and the older woman refused to tell. "You have caused me nothing but trouble," Martha told Roberta. "Get out and stay out," as she ordered her daughter-in-law to step off of her front porch.[132]

One of Martha's stepdaughters, identified as Mrs. Walter H. Manges, told reporters, "My mother loved [Roberta's] children and it was her one great desire that they have a good environment and an education. That is why she refused to tell their mother where they were when she came demanding them." Mrs. Manges said her stepbrother Oliver and his wife, Roberta, had lived "a story of a tangled marriage, jealousy and hatred."[133]

"Our family troubles dated to 1928, not long after Ruby [what the family called Roberta] came into the family," Mrs. Manges said. "She always accused mother of interfering and meddling, she always called her 'the old woman,' and she always hated her. Mother never meddled. In fact, at one time she moved back to South Bend to get away from Oliver and Ruby in order that she would have no part in their difficulties."[134]

Police learned that Roberta had occasionally asked Martha for help with her two children, including asking her to buy them new clothes. "They were brought to mother without proper clothing other than the garments they were wearing, and mother and I sewed for three weeks to outfit them in order that Eugene could go to school," Mrs. Manges explained. "Within a few weeks Ruby came for them, said she was tired of my mother having them, and they went away. While we had them we knew nothing of Ruby's whereabouts, if the children had died, we couldn't have notified her."

An Episcopalian priest in South Bend had also been enlisted by Roberta in caring for her children. The priest believed Roberta had serious health problems and found the children "badly soiled."[135]

Family members said Oliver had taken the children away from Roberta after becoming convinced that his wife could not properly care for them. A graduate of the University of Notre Dame, he had followed his career to New York City but regularly visited family in Indiana.

The investigation also showed Martha, Oliver's mother, had become convinced that Roberta should be nowhere near her children. Her stepdaughter said, "Mother refused to tell her where the children are. If it is ever in our power to keep them away from her and in the custody of their father, we will do it. Ollie is giving them a good home and the right sort of care."[136]

Charged with first-degree murder, as she awaited trial, Roberta did not shy away from talking to reporters. From inside her cell at the St. Joseph County Jail, she begged authorities to give her just five minutes with her children. Asked if she would continue to fight to get her children back if she were acquitted, Roberta declared, "I'd move heaven and earth to find them. It is all there is in life for me now….I was willing to give all I had to get my youngsters back; but today, because I demanded them and in an insane moment shot their grandmother when she refused me, they are all eager and determined to brand me a murderer!"[137]

Concerned that she be allowed to see her children, but not from behind bars, Roberta added, "If I am not permitted to see them, if I fail in my determination to find them, then I care little what happens to me. I mean that sincerely. My one hope from life is to have them with me; if that is to be denied, nothing else matters. They can do what they want with me; life will be empty enough that I won't worry whether I keep it or not….I have committed but one crime, loving and wanting my children. But I will not sob. Newspapers want sensation, and they are getting it. But when I go on trial, I'll not shed tears to wring sympathy from a curious mob to help my situation."[138]

A dramatic trial unfolded in South Bend in the last week of June 1938 and ended in equally dramatic fashion, with jurors finding Roberta not guilty of murdering her mother-in-law based on "temporary insanity."

"Mrs. Roberta Watters rests today in the county jail with the hope of recovering her two children, whom she had not seen in more than two years, the echo of the dramatic final arguments hardly died out," the *South Bend Tribune* noted. Roberta's colorful defense attorney, Paul M. Butler, announced that his client was "the mother of mothers" and said it was

Oliver Watters who was to blame for his own mother's death, not Roberta. "This woman has not failed society, society had failed her. Society should be condemned, not her."[139]

The verdict of not guilty by reason of temporary insanity was reached in less than two hours of deliberation, and Roberta attempted to reach out and shake hands with jurors as they exited the courtroom but collapsed into the arms of a jail matron standing by. She was revived and taken back to the jail clinic for observation. The trial judge had to determine, however, whether Roberta's insanity meant she needed to be housed in a state mental hospital, and therefore, she remained jailed.

The judge later ruled that Roberta should be released, and she resumed her search for her children, focusing on New York City, where she knew Oliver worked and lived, finally finding him in May 1939. Hauled before a city court judge, Oliver refused to tell where his two children were and was ordered held in jail for thirty days to think it over.

"After being taken to jail, [Oliver] experienced a change of heart and offered to tell the court the whereabouts of the children provided the 30-day sentence is suspended," the *South Bend Tribune* reported.[140]

New York authorities continued to hold Oliver on a $5,000 bond, and he cooperated with Indiana authorities, who sought his return on charges of "child stealing" and "harboring a child out of the custody of a person legally entitled to custody." Oliver relented, and eventually, final custody was awarded to Roberta, and the couple were granted a divorce in September 1939.

3

1940–49

ELWOOD'S ELUSIVE GUN GIRL

Fugitive(s): Isabelle Messmer
Wanted For: April 8, 1940, escape, Ector County Jail, Odessa, Texas
Captured: May 29, 1940, Tipton, Indiana

On the day she was captured exiting a movie theater in quiet Tipton, Indiana, on May 29, 1940, Isabelle Messmer was not a wanted fugitive in Indiana, but she might as well have been.

For years, Messmer (known to most as "Elwood's Gun Girl") captured headlines across the state and nation. On the run from authorities several times in her career, Messmer often returned to her mother's small wood-frame home at 227 North Seventh Street in Elwood to hide from authorities. Her trip back home to Indiana in the spring of 1940, however, aided in her capture.

In 1940, residents of Elwood were much more interested in being known for another of their own, Wendell L. Willkie, who, on June 28, 1940, was formally nominated by the Republican Party as its candidate for president of the United States. The leaders of Elwood were excited about the fame and notice Willkie's presence on the national stage would bring to the city, but then there were the pesky details of the Elwood Gun Girl that just wouldn't seem to go away.

Messmer, twenty-four, had helped put Elwood on the map but for all the wrong reasons. The only good thing most locals could say about her was that she kept most of her criminal activity far away from Elwood and was loyal in visiting her mother back home.

Her latest troubles began during the early morning hours of April 8, 1940, as Messmer escaped from the hospital ward of the Ector County Jail in Odessa, Texas, where she was being held on a three-year sentence for murder. She was convicted for the March 29, 1939 murder of Buford "Army" Armstrong, an "ace pitcher" for the House of David baseball team. A day before Messmer's escape, an Ector County judge had rejected an appeal of her murder conviction.

"The murderess made her escape after a county health officer failed to lock a lever box to the hospital cell door after taking her supper to her on Sunday night," officials told the *Odessa American*. "Her escape from the courthouse was made from the window on the west side. There are no bars on that window, and it leads to the ornate lattice decorations on the building, on which Miss Messmer descended as far as the first floor. She evidently leaped from the bottom the lattice to the ground."[141]

Messmer had always made a point of attracting a lot of media attention, eagerly talking to reporters and posing for photographs. In fact, she was so enamored of the media coverage she received that Isabelle and her mother kept a scrapbook of newspaper clippings of her exploits.

She hadn't always been bad. In 1930, the *Elwood Call Leader* listed her name among a group of students at Elwood Senior High School who completed an eight-week Bible class.[142] After that, though, things changed, and Isabelle dropped out of high school. In 1931, locals could get a sense that a rambunctious life was about to unfold, after a local article noted that she was a sixteen-year-old girl abandoned in Ohio by an unnamed male escort who had offered her an invitation to travel with him.[143]

Messmer really made the big time in October 1933, when reports from Pittsburgh were moved via the Associated Press wire, noting that the eighteen-year-old Elwood girl was arrested while carrying two guns and fought with police.

"Why shouldn't a girl tote a gun, especially if she's only 18 and weighs less than 100 and is very, very attractive?" The *Pittsburgh Sun-Telegraph* asked its readers next to a three-column photo of a sneering Messmer pointing a gun at the camera. "Why wouldn't she carry two pistols, even? A girl has to have protection these days. That's Isabelle Messmer's angle." The story included details, however, that "the little lady from Elwood, Indiana kicked and screamed at city detectives who arrested her. They were not at all surprised to learn that Isabelle was a tap dancer with a carnival, her nimble feet are very nimble."[144]

Isabelle's antics did not go unnoticed back home. The *Elwood Call Leader* reported on her arrest and noted, "The young woman is said to have thrown the [Pittsburgh] detective bureau into an uproar, frustrating efforts to photograph or fingerprint her, and aimed savage kicks and blows at officers."[145]

A Pennsylvania judge later gave Messmer a one-year suspended sentence with the understanding that she was not to return to the state, ever.[146]

True to her word, Messmer stayed out of Pennsylvania but just a month later was under arrest again, this time in Miami, Florida, on a charge of carrying a gun and robbing "a prominent Miami resident" of $900.[147] Released on bond, Messmer was arrested again less than a week later, on February 7, 1934, after a Miami policeman said she drew an automatic pistol on him when he approached her.[148] She was eventually ordered to be held for thirty days in Miami.[149]

Less than six months later, in August 1934, police in Washington, D.C., reported that they had arrested Messmer on multiple charges related to robberies in the nation's capital. Interestingly, police said they nabbed Messmer outside a downtown hotel while she was dressed as a boy. At the time, D.C. police were seeking a dark-haired woman as a suspect. "Although attired in a blue shirt, white cap, white duck trousers and white shoes, Isabelle was betrayed in her disguise by a little wisp of black hair protruding from beneath her blonde wig."[150]

The Associated Press reported that Messmer, using the alias "Joyce Palmer," admitted she had traveled freely to thirty-eight states in the United States since she was fifteen years old. "Her parents, separated, did not object to her departure and that she still receives an allowance from one of them," the AP noted. "They've got nothing on me 'cept that I was wearing boy's pants and had a pistol in my room," Messmer told curious reporters. "They gotta let me go."[151]

A day after her arrest, the *New York Daily News* featured two photographs of a smiling Messmer, one in her boy's attire, and another in a pretty dress as a young woman. The *Daily News* noted, "This little girl almost fooled police of Washington by disguising herself as a boy and then as a blonde with long curls."[152] She eventually was sentenced to serve sixty days in jail at Washington, D.C., on a charge of passing $400 in bogus checks.

Released from jail, Messmer returned to Florida. In March 1936, she was arrested again on a charge of vagrancy, an all-inclusive charge police often used to run off characters they wanted no part of. Picked up in a tourist campground, Messmer once again happily smiled for news photographers as she was fingerprinted by Miami police.[153]

Messmer struggled to stay out of trouble, as evidenced by her June 1937 arrest in Washington, D.C., again on suspicion of passing bogus checks. "The Elwood, Indiana girl with the tantalizing smile and rolling brown eyes more expressive than those of a movie star" was back in police custody, "but today, her nonchalant air was gone. She shed bitter tears and she stood… waiting for the [police] wagon and actually appeared embarrassed by the staring crowd that gathered about her. She was so unlike Isabelle as this town has known her," a dispatch printed in the *Indianapolis Star* noted.[154]

One Washington, D.C. reporter noted that "Isabelle has been a girl who liked to show off; she is a dramatic type. She was always 'acting' when she was an Elwood High School girl. Dumb police once again thought of her as a mental case—they decided she is a mental case in the sense that she is plenty smart, smarter than most policemen.…Heretofore, she has rather enjoyed her exploits with the police, and especially some newspaper attention for she keeps a scrapbook."[155]

Somehow working herself free of the legal entanglements in Washington, D.C., Messmer next popped up in Newark, New Jersey, in October 1938, where she was charged again with a check-writing scam. When sentencing Messmer to the women's reformatory at Clinton, New Jersey, Essex County judge Richard Hartshorne told her that her days of "relying on a pretty face" were over. The judge ignored her emotional outbursts, demanding that she be returned to her mother in Indiana.[156]

Messmer and another woman escaped from the New Jersey facility on January 20, 1939, and she made her way to Texas oil country. The *New York Daily News* reported, "She learned that the oil field workers around Odessa made good money and were free spenders, so she followed the advice of a woman hitchhiker and rented a tourist cabin. As she phrased it, 'I set myself up in a quiet little business. I liked the oil field workers and the ranchers.'"[157]

Her newfound profession of entertaining working men for money ran afoul, however, in March 1940, when one man, the semipro baseball pitcher Buford Armstrong, didn't want to pay for his fun. A fight ensued, and Armstrong lost. His lifeless body was found hours later inside Messmer's now abandoned cabin.

She was later convicted for Armstrong's murder but was again a free woman after escaping the Odessa jail. Police in Indiana were on the lookout for Isabelle on the chance she might want to come home for a visit. Indiana newspaper readers were also following the story of the Elwood Gun Girl closely and knew what she looked like. Among those was an Elwood man in Tipton on business on May 29, 1940. Believing he spotted Messmer exiting a bus and then entering the Ritz Theatre, the police were notified, and they waited for the film to end and arrested her.[158]

After less than a week at the Tipton County Jail while extradition issues were resolved between Texas and New Jersey for Messmer's custody, Tipton County sheriff Richard Hobbs said he was more than eager to transfer his prisoner. Hobbs reported that Messmer had attempted to choke her mother when she visited her at the jail and threw the elderly woman to the floor of her jail cell.

"When the Sheriff elected to put Miss Messmer in a solitary cell, she pelted him with dishes and slashed at him with a razor blade," the Associated Press reported. "She missed [cutting the sheriff] but accidentally cut her own wrist. Next she began taking off her clothing and the sheriff, two deputies and a state trooper had to help subdue her." Witnesses reported Messmer screamed, "I'll kill someone yet before it's all over!"[159]

Messmer's mother, Ethel Decker of Elwood, was attempting to get an insanity order entered for her daughter to allow her to remain in Indiana for treatment rather than to return to jail in Texas or New Jersey. Petitions she filed in both Tipton and Madison counties were denied.

The Ector County sheriff arrived in Tipton from Texas, determined to take Messmer back with him. Indiana authorities were cooperating, but Isabelle wasn't going without a fight.

"Calling repeatedly for her mother, whom she is said to have tried to strangle a day earlier, [Isabelle] shrieked out the last chapter of her sojourn in jail [in Tipton] when she was loaded in a state police car, bound for the Indianapolis airport," the Associated Press reported. "Manacled with handcuffs and leg irons, the erstwhile 'Elwood Gun Girl' shrieked threats to kill, screamed that she wanted her mother, and fought Sheriff Hobbs." Once they got her in the state police car, reporters witnessed Messmer "screaming with maniacal fury" as she "threw herself at the sheriff in the backseat with imprecations and threats to kill." A sedative given to her by the Tipton County health officer apparently was having no effect.[160]

"At the Indianapolis airport, the Texas sheriff, wearing a sombrero, cowboy boots and his pistol stuffed in his belt, was accustomed to chasing Isabelle around the country," the *Elwood Call Leader* indicated. Sheriff Webb of Ector County was overhead joking with Isabelle, telling her, "You ought to feel lucky getting off with three years," which was her original sentence for the murder. His words appeared to console her, it was noted.[161]

Messmer was infuriated again, however, once the plane carrying her back to Texas landed at Odessa. Reporters noted the ninety-five-pound woman had to be subdued in a similar manner as before, with several officers required to pin her down to the back seat of a police car.

Returned to the Ector County Jail to complete her sentence (and additional time for escape), Messmer amazingly slipped out of the jail again—the second time in eight months—on November 11, 1940. For the second time, Ector County jailers had left her jail cell unlocked, and she again worked her way down the side of the courthouse jail from the third floor and ran away.[162]

An intense search was undertaken, and in March 1941, police surrounded the Elwood home of Messmer's mother, Ethel Decker, after a witness reported seeing her get off a bus in Muncie and order a taxi to take her to Elwood. If Isabelle was present that day, she got away, as police made no arrest.[163]

Finally, on April 22, 1940, San Francisco police reported they had Messmer under arrest in their city. Once in custody, she confirmed she *had* been in Elwood a month earlier and somehow managed to escape out a back door as six police officers approached her mother's home.[164] During an extradition hearing in San Francisco, Messmer acted out violently, striking an elderly jail matron before being subdued.

Returned to Odessa once again, Ector County officials decided to transfer Messmer to the custody of the state prison system to ensure she stayed in place this time. Vowing to be "a good girl from now on," Messmer served the rest of her Texas sentence without incident. In December 1942, she was turned over to New Jersey authorities to answer for her earlier escape there. She received a short sentence there for escape and was later released.

From there, Messmer dropped out of the news, although she made an appearance again by entering an interracial marriage with a Black Indianapolis man in 1951 and attempted to settle down in Noblesville. Apparently stymied by locals who did not approve of interracial marriages, Messmer divorced and moved to Florida in 1963, where she married again. Messmer died in 1984 at the age of seventy.[165]

NEVADA EXECUTES SEVENTEEN-YEAR-OLD INDIANA FUGITIVE

Fugitive(s): Floyd Burton Loveless and Dale Cline
Wanted For: August 16, 1942, escape, Indiana Boys' School, Plainfield, Indiana
Captured: August 20, 1942, Elko, Nevada

In the short period from July to October 1942, fifteen-year-old Floyd Burton Loveless went from a small-time burglar in Lafayette, Indiana, to a condemned man on Nevada's death row.

The State of Nevada eventually had its way, placing Loveless in the gas chamber at the age of seventeen, where he died on September 29, 1944. The path leading from the rough-and-tumble life Loveless had known as a boy in the rural areas of Tippecanoe County to the gas chamber was astonishingly short.

Well known to local police, Loveless finally faced the music for his most serious crimes in July 1942, when he was charged in a series of home burglaries and assaults on women in the Lafayette area. Loveless grew up in Clarks Hill, a small settlement about fifteen miles southeast of the county seat. Newspaper reporters quickly dubbed him the "most dangerous criminal the local police have encountered in recent years." The *Lafayette Journal & Courier* spared no drama in describing the crimes alleged against Loveless: "The depredations of the cat-like burglar have caused a reign of terror, and his arrest and confession Monday evening, after more than two weeks of clever, painstaking and untiring work by the police, will restore peace of mind in the ranks of local housewives."[166]

Loveless was arrested along with his seventeen-year-old brother, Robert K. Loveless, who allegedly admitted he attempted to sell a gun and wristwatch stolen by his brother from a home at 417 Park Avenue in Lafayette. The woman at home at the time of the burglary, identified as Mrs. Francis Knoth in newspaper accounts, was also assaulted.

"Both youths were already on probation, authorities said, [and] Floyd was put on probation last December after burglarizing a Laramie Township home and was held in jail for nine days," reported the *Lafayette Journal & Courier*. His brother, Robert, was previously arrested on a vehicle theft charge.[167]

Newspaper reports about the Loveless brothers indicated perhaps why they were running afoul of the law—they were essentially on their own. Their mother was reportedly killed in a car-train crash in 1930, and their father had moved to Fort Wayne for work and left them in the care of a family relative.

The current slate of crimes attributed to Floyd, however, caused many in the community to lose any sense of compassion they might have had for him based on his youth. In one case, Floyd was accused of breaking into the West Kossuth Street home of Mary Soller and assaulting her and "nearly killing her with a milk bottle." Floyd admitted invading both homes, "robbing Mrs. Soller of $40 and taking a gun and watch from the Knoth home," the *Journal & Courier* relayed. "Robert admitted receiving $20 of the Soller loot and the gun and watch, both of which have been recovered."[168]

Tracing the watch that the boys attempted to sell was key in tracking them down. A fingerprint taken from the milk bottle used to batter Mrs. Soller also matched Floyd.

Before the Lovelesses were apprehended, Floyd admitted that he had stolen three cars in town, including one taken from a family on July 4 while they watched Independence Day fireworks at Columbian Park in Lafayette. He later abandoned both cars but admitted that he had successfully resold several bicycles that he stole from outside Lafayette homes, stores and movie theaters.

Three days after his arrest, Floyd Loveless was sentenced by Tippecanoe County Juvenile Court judge W. Lynn Parkinson to the Indiana Boys' School at Plainfield for a term of six years—or until he was twenty-one years old. Robert Loveless was given a sentence of five years at the Pendleton Reformatory for his part in the crimes.[169]

Reporters later concluded what many in the community already had: "While Loveless is acknowledged to be a dangerous criminal of the worst type, his tender age saved him from a long prison term [in Indiana] as under the law authorities could not send such a young person to the penitentiary."[170]

Floyd Loveless did not intend to stay in jail, it seems, as less than a month after being sentenced to the Boys' School, he escaped (gone six hours before officials discovered his delivery from the institution). Also slipping away with Loveless was a boy identified at Dale Cline, fifteen.[171]

The flight of freedom for Loveless and Cline was short-lived but ended in a spectacular and deadly fashion more than 1,700 miles west of Plainfield at tiny Elko, Nevada, a dusty desert town in northeast Nevada. On August 20, 1942, Elko County sheriff C.A. Harper reported that he had both boys in custody but not before a high-speed auto chase in which a local constable was seriously wounded after being shot at point-blank range by Loveless as the officer attempted to remove him from a stolen truck.

Cline was captured fifteen miles west of Elko as he drove a stolen car trying to get away. He gave up after sheriff's deputies fired a shotgun blast at the car, shattering its windshield. Cline was not injured.

Loveless was arrested nine miles west of Elko in an area known as Emigrant Pass. Loveless's arrest, however, did not come before he wounded A.W. Berning, the constable of Carlin, a town at the edge of the Rocky Mountains and the Emigrant Pass into California. The investigation showed that, curiously, after shooting Berning, Loveless dragged the officer's body to the truck and placed him in the passenger seat and continued to flee.

Constable Berning's wounds were described as serious, and newspaper reports indicated that he was paralyzed from the neck down as a result of a bullet wound in his neck and a second bullet lodged in his groin. "He was growing steadily worse this afternoon," the *Reno Gazette-Journal* reported about the officer's condition. "Hospital attaches expressed grave fears that he will not recover."[172]

Berning was shot as he attempted to stop Loveless in a stolen truck carrying Indiana license plates swiped from an employee parking lot at the Boys' School in Plainfield three days earlier. Sheriff Harper said the boys arrived together in Elko in the stolen truck but started to argue, which caused Cline to set out on his own and steal a separate vehicle outside a local ranch.

Loveless, who by shooting Berning was able to get away, abandoned the truck "and left Berning wounded, bleeding and unconscious inside the vehicle. Loveless started to hitchhike in a last dash for freedom." The grave concerns about Berning's injuries proved accurate, as he succumbed to them during the early morning hours of August 22, 1942. As a result, "Elko County authorities, with the full backing of a thoroughly aroused community, are determined to exact the full penalty of the law from his 15-year-old slayer," the *Reno Gazette-Journal* noted. At the time of his death at the age of fifty-six, Berning was one of Nevada's longest-serving constables, having started his duties in 1916.[173]

Nevada officials were true to their word, trying Loveless on a charge of first-degree murder as an adult, with a jury finding him guilty on October 1, 1942 (just ninety days after he was originally arrested in Indiana). "The death sentence will be mandatory because the jury made no recommendation for leniency," United Press reported in a story gaining national attention because of the novelty of a fifteen-year-old facing the gas chamber.[174]

As expected, numerous appeals for clemency or a reduced sentence for Loveless delayed his original execution scheduled for December 1942. By September 1944, only a pardon or sentence commutation from Nevada governor Edward P. Carville could save Loveless's life. The governor faced a tough decision—media attention on Loveless had continued while he was held in the state prison at Carson City. One newspaper report stated, "Loveless is a star pitcher and third basement on the prison softball team."[175]

Reno attorneys Royal Stewart and Bert Goldwater continued to try to win a stay of execution for Loveless, arguing before the Nevada Supreme Court that a fuller examination of Loveless's mental state was needed before the execution could proceed. Their claim that Loveless was insane when he shot Constable Berning delayed but did not stop the execution process.

By the close of September 1944, the end was near. "Loveless, the youngest person to die in the Nevada gas execution chamber, located in the middle of the state prison yard," was in his last hours of life on September 29, 1944. "Last night, preparing himself for the scheduled execution, Loveless spent several hours with a priest. Father Buell of Gardnerville said Loveless embraced Catholicism in the last few months. His last requests were to have the warden send roses to his grandmother in Indiana, and that his personal belongings be given to a prison friend."[176]

AN OLD FUGITIVE FORMS A NEW LIFE IN CALIFORNIA

Fugitive(s): James J. Taylor
Wanted For: October 23, 1919, escape, Indiana State Prison, Michigan City, Indiana
Captured: June 2, 1943, Hawthorne, California

For twenty-three years, it seemed James J. Taylor was free and clear, a fugitive from the Indiana State Prison, until a routine traffic stop in Hawthorne, California, brought his long run of freedom to an end.

Taylor, a well-liked fifty-five-year-old man known to everyone as Charles A. Proctor, wasn't exactly running from authorities. He walked away from the prison on October 23, 1919 (where he was serving a sentence for the murder of his stepbrother), and Indiana authorities had no idea where he was, though he had put down roots and started a new life in Southern California.

The traffic stop, just after Memorial Day 1943, found Taylor charged with driving while under the influence. Police released him but also followed their normal procedure of sending his fingerprints along to the FBI in Washington, D.C. The FBI gave notice that Taylor was wanted in Indiana.

Once confronted with the truth about his identity, "broken and tearful, Taylor confessed he was a fugitive from an Indiana prison who had escaped to California and had been living here ever since under an assumed name," the *Los Angeles Times* reported. During his time in Los Angeles, Taylor had married a divorced mother of two in 1926. His wife, Nellie, "was stunned by the tragic turn of events. She said she never suspected her husband, who was employed as a construction manager by a Redondo Beach building contractor."[177]

Nellie told reporters that her husband had provided for her son and daughter from her previous marriage and secured a good home for the family in Lennox (a small community nestled between Inglewood and Hawthorne in Los Angeles County). "He was a model husband in every sense of the word," Nellie told a reporter between deep sobs. "He raised my two children by my first marriage as his own, and there was never a kinder husband and father." Mrs. Taylor took issue with any effort to hold her husband accountable to his original charges. "I know the law must be served," she said, "but it seems a shame in this case."[178]

Taylor defended himself against the original charges that sent him to prison. "I was accused of killing my stepbrother, but I never really knew whether I did or not," Taylor said. "My father, my stepbrother and myself had been drinking at a party. My stepbrother had won a shotgun as some kind of a prize and when we went home I remember him starting to put the gun in a closet. It went off and he was killed. My stepmother blamed me and I took the rap."[179]

Back in Indiana, the Indiana State Prison board voted to ask Governor Henry F. Schricker to issue extradition papers for Taylor's return. At the same time, more than five hundred letters from businessmen, neighbors and friends of Taylor were forwarded to California governor Earl Warren, asking him to deny any extradition request from Indiana. Taylor's attorney, Charles L. Blek, said the letters would prove that although he was a fugitive from prison, he was also a fully rehabilitated, law-abiding citizen.[180]

Further helping Taylor's effort to remain in California instead of having to go back to prison in Indiana was a telegram Blek showed reporters from the former Pike County prosecutor Harry W. Carpenter, who had prosecuted the original 1919 case against Taylor. The telegram said, "If I can help you in any way, let me know." Blek said Carpenter had told him by telephone that he "saw no reason" why Taylor should be returned to prison based on his stellar record since his escape.[181]

Carpenter led the case against Taylor for the February 16, 1919 incident in which his sixteen-year-old stepbrother, Wesley Taylor, died. "It is charged that the death was the result of a family feud, in which James Taylor desired to kill his stepmother, but in the darkness shot and killed his stepbrother instead."[182]

On June 28, 1943, the California governor officially denied the extradition application from Indiana and ordered that Taylor remain in California. The desire to return Taylor to Indiana appeared to be waning. An Associated Press reporter from Sacramento reached Indiana Governor Schricker on the telephone and told him his application was being denied before he had been officially informed. Schricker remarked, "That's up to the California officials. If they want to keep him, that's all right with me."[183]

The Los Angeles County Jail released Taylor officially on June 29, 1943, noting that he would remain free as long as he never entered Indiana. "I Love You, California!" Taylor sang as he stepped from the jail before reporters. One reporter asked if he would ever again sing "Back Home Again, in Indiana." He replied, "Well, I don't plan to go back there for a vacation soon."[184]

While newspapers across the nation were quick to run a photograph of Mrs. Taylor weeping and clinging to her husband's neck as she considered that he would go back to prison, they also ran a photo of the smiling couple on August 13, 1943. On that day, Taylor went to court to have his name officially changed to Charles A. Proctor and tried to put his past behind him once and for all.[185]

4

1950–59

A FUGITIVE TURNS INTO A KILLER

Fugitive(s): William J. Townsend
Wanted For: June 5, 1953, escape, Indiana Reformatory, Pendleton, Indiana
July 17, 1953, murder, Kansas City, Missouri
Captured: August 22, 1953, Logansport, Indiana

An old yarn suggesting that the worst children are those born of ministers and police officers certainly held true in the case of William J. Townsend, twenty-three.

Townsend, son of a Pentecostal minister in Logansport, was sentenced to two- to twenty-one years in prison for the rape of a fifteen-year-old Huntington County girl in 1949. He was four years into his sentence when he and three other men escaped the Indiana Reformatory at Pendleton on June 5, 1953.[186]

Described as a freckle-faced redhead and a slight young man of just 133 pounds, Townsend was the only one of the escaping quartet who remained at large for any length of time. Police in Cass and Fulton Counties were advised to be on the lookout for Townsend, who they thought would come home to seek the help of his father. They were way off.[187]

Townsend made his way south from Pendleton to Louisville, Kentucky, and eventually settled for about a month on the run in St. Louis, Missouri. Townsend, living under the alias of Rocky Jackson, remained in Missouri until fleeing back home to Logansport in late August 1953—and his two months of freedom came to an end.

His apprehension in Logansport was not the work of local authorities but instead Missouri detectives and the FBI. Back in St. Louis, police questioned a married nineteen-year-old woman, Clara Lyston, about her association with alleged car thieves. She disclosed little useful information about the car thieves but did say she had made the association of Rocky Jackson, who had confessed to her he had killed a priest.

"Mrs. Lyston said Townsend told her he had been hitchhiking in Kansas City and the priest gave him a ride," the *St. Louis Globe-Democrat* reported. She also revealed the man she knew as "Rocky" had the priest's driver's license and other personal papers in his possession.[188]

St. Louis authorities quickly notified police in Kansas City and learned they had an open death investigation involving the Reverend Robert A. Hodges, thirty-six, a chaplain at St. Joseph's Hospital in Kansas City. Father Hodges's body was found on July 17, 1953, about a mile south of U.S. 40, near the Little Blue River, east of Kansas City. He had suffered a fatal gunshot wound.

His body was positively identified by the vice-chancellor of the Kansas City diocese, and police learned that he was a priest, despite Hodges being dressed in casual clothing. Cleric's clothing was found later in Hodges's car abandoned a short distance away. Hodges, who had been missing for two days before his body was found, had been a priest for a dozen years and the last two as a hospital chaplain.[189]

At the time Hodges's body was found, the local sheriff declared that he believed the death to be accidental, the man shot by a hunter. That theory remained the conclusion in the death of Father Hodges until Townsend implicated himself.

Mrs. Lyston, Townsend's St. Louis acquaintance, said she believed her friend was headed back to Logansport, Indiana. At about the same time, "a motorist in a tavern in Logansport told the bartender he had just accommodated a hitchhiker who appeared extremely nervous. The bartender informed the police, and federal agents and state officers made the arrest."[190]

Police found Townsend hiding in a small camper on the property of his embarrassed father, the Reverend Shelby Townsend. He was unarmed and offered no resistance when arrested on August 22, 1953.

Once under arrest, Townsend was transferred to the St. Joseph County Jail at South Bend and under fifteen hours of intense questioning by detectives, confessed to killing Father Hodges in Missouri. The priest's rosary was among the items recovered from Townsend's pockets.

Townsend explained that the priest had picked him up as he was hitchhiking along U.S. 40 outside of Kansas City and then drove to a remote area. Once there, Townsend said, Hodges made "homosexual advances" on him, and he shot him. Townsend asserted that "the priest, wearing a sport shirt, picked him up outside Kansas City and made indecent advances until 'I was mad and cursing him,'" the *Logansport Pharos-Tribune* relayed. "Townsend claimed that the Rev. Hodges talked him into leaving the car to go to a cottage on a river bank, but while walking through brush, he was struck by a tree limb, and 'I became madder than ever.'"[191]

In his formal statement to police, Townsend said he began to believe there was no river cottage nearby, and that the priest had struck him with the limb. "This made me so mad I pulled the gun from my belt and I started shooting. I don't know how many times I fired....The next thing I remember, I was walking down the highway and it was raining. I had my revolver in my right hand and a beaded rosary in my left hand."[192]

He admitted he had taken Hodges's wallet containing thirteen dollars and only then, when looking through the contents of it, learned that he was a member of the clergy.

Four days after his arrest, and held on a large bond of $50,000, Townsend waived extradition and was transported from South Bend to Kansas City via airplane. Townsend was scheduled to go on trial in November 1953, but a week before the trial was to start, he agreed to plead guilty to a charge of murder, with the auto theft charges dropped. Judge John R. James sentenced Townsend to life in the Missouri State Prison.[193]

THICK EYEGLASSES GIVE AWAY AN INDIANA FUGITIVE

Fugitive(s): John Paul Jameson and Harvey Girtch
Wanted For: January 5, 1954, escape, Indiana State Penal Farm, Westville, Indiana
Captured: February 18, 1954, Phoenix, Arizona

Physical descriptions of wanted fugitives are often the key to rounding them up, and that proved to be the case in the capture of convicted Indiana murderer and prison escapee John Paul Jameson on February 18, 1954.

Jameson, forty-two, and Harvey Girtch, forty-eight, were both escapees from the Indiana State Prison Farm in LaPorte County when rounded up by an observant police officer in Phoenix, Arizona. More than 1,700 miles from where they had slipped away, it was Jameson's thick eyeglasses that stood out to Patrolman Robert Flack.

"I was in my patrol car," Flack said. "I saw this car with three men in it pull out of a service station….They looked the right age to be the escapees, and one of them wore glasses." Police in Phoenix had been asked to be on the lookout for the men after a tip was received in Indiana that they were hitchhiking their way west to that city. Flack said he had not seen a photograph of the men but had only read a description that included mention of the thick eyeglasses and remembered it while on his routine patrol.[194]

A third man detained with Jameson and Girtch was questioned but released after it was determined that he was not wanted. Flack said Jameson and Girtch presented identification cards but could not remember the names on them. "They fumbled around before they answered," Flack said, raising his suspicion even further.[195]

En route to being questioned at the Phoenix police headquarters, Jameson and Girtch admitted they were wanted in Indiana and were driving a car they had stolen in South Bend. Both men said they walked away from a work detail on January 5, 1954, and had been moving west across the country ever since.

Back at the State Prison Farm near Westville in LaPorte County, the investigation showed how the two had managed their escape. Jameson and Girtch were assigned the duty of setting up and running a film projector for other inmates, and once the film was started, they slipped away. "Nobody knew they were gone until the reel needed changing," said state probation officer Bert Rudicel. Rudicel said both men had been granted "trustee" status because of their good behavior behind bars.[196]

Granting trustee status to Jameson, it seemed, was a poorly considered option, given his violent and slippery past of evading the police and refusing to remain behind bars. Girtch, held on a theft conspiracy charge, had no record of violence. Jameson was another matter. In just over a dozen years since Jameson was sentenced to life in prison on July 7, 1941, he had won over prison officials as a trustworthy man. A careful review of his record reveals that it was a misplaced trust.

Jameson's name was a familiar one to Indianapolis authorities, the case that sent him to prison for life having made headlines throughout the spring and summer of 1940. Jameson was officially charged with the execution-type slaying of Howard Priest, twenty-eight, of Indianapolis, whose body was found dumped in a gravel pit near Broad Ripple on May 27, 1940. At the time of the May 1940 shooting, Jameson had only been free from prison from previous charges for seven months.

Priest and his wife, Gertrude, twenty-two, had rented a room in their home at 1318 Carrollton Avenue to Jameson. An investigation shows that Jameson pursued a romantic interest in Gertrude Priest, despite her being a married woman, and an argument ensued between the two men.

"Authorities believed Priest was slain and [immediately] discounted a theory of suicide because no weapon was found at the scene," the *Indianapolis News* reported. Priest's body was found about three hundred yards east of Westfield Boulevard at the American Aggregates Corporation gravel pit. An autopsy showed he was shot through the heart with a .32-caliber weapon pressed against his chest.[197]

Although it appeared that one of Priest's pockets had been checked for money and his wallet was missing, five ten-dollar bills were found in a watch case on his person. Robbery, however, was an early theory before police began closely questioning Gertrude Priest. That intense questioning included holding her (and another tenant of her home) on a general charge of vagrancy. In fact, Mrs. Priest was held in the Marion County Jail, and although she was allowed to view her husband's body at the mortuary, she was whisked back to the jail and forbidden to attend his funeral.[198]

Media reports never made clear whether Mrs. Priest and Jameson had actually consummated a relationship, although it appears police had problems with her account that her husband of four years left in a taxicab at 10:00 p.m. on Sunday evening, May 25, 1940, and never returned. She left out the detail that he had left the home in Jameson's company—a fact later revealed by an Indianapolis taxicab driver who said the two men were drinking in his cab and were dropped off in the 6700 block of Westfield Boulevard, near the White River bridge.[199]

Mrs. Priest was eventually released by police and not charged with any crime, as police were not convinced that she (or the other man staying at her home) had anything to do with the murder of Howard Priest.

In an odd twist in the case, Gertrude Priest's attractive image was splashed in newspaper advertisements placed in Indianapolis and elsewhere for the latest edition of *Actual Detective Stories*, a racy true-crime magazine published nationally between 1937 and 1943. The advertisement asked the question in a bold headline over Mrs. Priest's picture: "Indianapolis Wife Asks: Why the Chair for Me?" The story (published in the October 1940 edition of the magazine) promised for just fifteen cents a copy of the "surprising developments" and "dark facts" in the story of Mrs. Priest, who police were convinced had helped in killing her husband.[200]

"What did Mrs. Priest know? What other startling events preceded the discovery of Mr. Priest's body in the gravel pit? Mrs. Priest tells in her own words what it feels like to be a murder suspect—the horrible feeling of being trapped in a tight web of circumstantial evidence."[201]

Despite whatever misgivings Mrs. Priest might have had about the hardball tactics of the police, they paid off as Marion County sheriff Al Feeney announced that he had received a criminal indictment for Jameson, who was at large. "A 'triangle' affair, involving Priest's wife, may have been the motive behind the slaying," Feeney indicated. News media reports indicated that Feeney and his men had "been working steadily for 24 hours without rest," and Feeney offered without explanation, "We have an eyewitness to the murder" (presumably the taxicab driver), identified as Virgil Betts.[202]

As Jameson's picture was blasted across the daily newspapers in Indianapolis, he fled. Investigators believed he robbed a Perry Township couple of $600 in cash on a downtown street before taking a brand-new 1940 automobile being chauffeured for a prominent Indianapolis businessman. In both cases, the victims stated their assailant was a well-dressed man in a business suit wearing thick eyeglasses.[203]

About a month later, on June 23, 1940, police in Montgomery County, acting on a report of a suspicious man staying at a remote cabin near Sugar Creek (northwest of Crawfordsville), attempted a raid to arrest the man believed to be Jameson. The raid didn't go well. "Jameson escaped a salvo of gunfire early yesterday morning from a raiding party that surprised him at a woodland cabin," the *Indianapolis Star* reported. "Directed by airplane, Montgomery County authorities ranged fields and woodlands of western Indiana all day in a search for Jameson. Illinois authorities were also asked to watch along the state line for the fugitive."[204]

The raiding party included four Crawfordsville policemen, two Indiana State Police troopers, Montgomery County sheriff Harold Roth and the state parole officer, William Purdue, who almost succeeded in capturing their man. They snuck up on Jameson under the cover of darkness at around 1:30 a.m. as Jameson was spotted "sitting quietly in the darkness of a summer cottage porch."[205]

Crawfordsville Police captain Otto Biederstedt said he ordered Jameson to surrender. "But instead of complying with the order, Jameson leaped to his feet, drew a gun and fired six times. None in the raiding squad was struck," an account in the *Indianapolis Star* said.[206]

Jameson jumped from the porch and ran into a thicket along Sugar Creek, Biederstedt said, "with 30 to 40 shots being fired by the raiding party." Police believed they had not wounded Jameson, however. He remained at large another month, until a semitruck was stopped outside Terre Haute by a Vigo County sheriff's deputy on July 22, 1940. The deputy, Horace Barnard, said he saw a man matching Jameson's description with eyeglasses on but now sporting a mustache. As Barnard attempted to question the driver of the truck and his passenger (Jameson), Jameson jumped from the truck and attempted to shoot Deputy Barnard. His gun did not fire, however, and he ran to a nearby field to hide and was quickly apprehended.

Once in custody, it was discovered that Jameson had been struck by the barrage of bullets fired at him near Crawfordsville a month earlier. He had attempted to self-treat a grazing wound to his head with alcohol and bandages and was nearly healed, but a bullet remained lodged painfully in his ankle, greatly reducing his ability to walk or run.[207]

Indianapolis police were happy to put Jameson on display in their custody, and preparations were to begin immediately for a murder trial. In a written statement, Jameson said he and Priest had quarreled many times in the past and that he had shot Priest in self-defense.

In the intervening days, however, Jameson's attorneys won a motion to move his case to Hendricks County. As he healed from his ankle wound, Jameson apparently hatched new ideas about escape. On April 20, 1941, as Hendricks County sheriff John Dent attempted to serve breakfast at the Greenfield jail, Jameson attacked.

Fashioning a homemade "blackjack" improvised from iron from a jail mop and friction tape, Jameson struck Sheriff Dent violently over the head. The Greenfield jail, which did not contain traditional cells but instead holding rooms, allowed Jameson to hide behind a door and get the jump on the sheriff.

"Jameson struck the sheriff on the head with the improvised blackjack, and the two men went to the floor fighting," the *Indianapolis Star* reported. Sheriff Dent's wife, "attracted by noise of the scuffle, locked doors leading to the outside and rushed to her husband's aid. As Jameson struck the sheriff blow after blow with the blackjack, Mrs. Dent seized the prisoner by the hair and attempted to pull him away."[208]

As the battle to control Jameson continued, the sheriff's daughter, twenty-five-year-old Carrie Dell Dent, grabbed a gun from her father's desk and pointed it at Jameson. She did not fire for fear of striking Jameson, but as he broke free, Sheriff Dent took the gun and fired in his direction. Jameson was not struck but surrendered in the sheriff's apartment, crying out, "Don't shoot! Don't shoot!"[209]

Suffering from a series of deep cuts on his head, Sheriff Dent was treated by a doctor at the scene, and Jameson was transferred immediately to the Indiana State Reformatory at Pendleton. He remained there until his trial, which was scheduled for early July 1941.

Despite all of the excitement leading up to his trial, it ended uneventfully just as a jury of twelve Hendricks County farmers were seated to hear the case. Judge John B. Hinchman accepted Jameson's change of plea—from not guilty to guilty—and promptly sentenced him to life in prison. It was from that life sentence that Jameson took one more flight of freedom in 1954.[210]

AN UNCEREMONIOUS END FOR LESLIE "MAD DOG" IRVIN

Fugitive(s): Leslie "Mad Dog" Irvin
Wanted For: January 19, 1956, escape, Gibson County Jail, Princeton, Indiana
Captured: February 9, 1956, San Francisco, California

Less than a month after he escaped the aging Gibson County Jail in Princeton, Leslie Irvin's fugitive trail ended unceremoniously on February 9, 1956, in a San Francisco pawn shop as he tried to hock a stolen diamond ring.

"Don't you know who I am?" Irvin asked detectives who detained him.

"I'm Leslie Irvin, and I'm wanted in Indiana for six murders," he reportedly told the San Francisco police officers as they were still attempting to determine his true identity. "I've been convicted of one and I'm not guilty of any." Reporters in San Francisco indicated that Irvin appeared five years younger than his age of thirty-one and described him as possessing "handsome crew cut looks."[211] At the time he was nabbed in California, Irvin was wanted in Indiana, where he had been convicted of one of six murders he allegedly committed. At the time of his arrest, Irvin had been in San Francisco only a day, having hitchhiked to the city from Los Angeles, where he had participated in several burglaries (including the one where he lifted the diamond ring he was trying to pawn).

"At the Hall of Justice [in San Francisco], Irvin sat slouched in a chair with his hands in his lap and answered reporters' questions in a low and unemotional voice," the AP reported. "He said he accomplished his incredible [Indiana] escape by fashioning two keys from layers of cardboard taken from the backs of paperbound novels he was allowed to have in his cell."[212]

Irvin said he had no formal training in locksmithing but made the keys from "just studying" the keys the guards used to open his cell. He reportedly made five attempts to make his cardboard key work, until it actually did. On the day he escaped, January 19, 1956, Irvin said he was aided by a heavy snowstorm that slowed any attempt by police to find him. Drivers in the area were friendly and readily gave rides to a hitchhiker needing a ride on a cold, snowy day.

"I tell you it felt good to get out," Irvin said. "But it was cold and snowing. It was about 8 o'clock when I left and it snowed all night. I wasn't but a few blocks away from the jail when I saw a city policeman in a patrol car looking at me in a funny way. He drove on by, but then started to turn around and I took off."[213]

Irvin claimed he walked thirteen miles from Princeton to the Indiana-Illinois state line before he was picked up by a driver.

Being a fugitive was not to Irvin's liking: "It was pretty tough. Every time somebody stopped us or maybe a waitress looked twice at you in a restaurant, you got jumpy." There was one big close call—a truck driver who had given Irvin a ride eventually recognized him from descriptions given on radio news reports. Irvin said he slipped out of a café and got away as the trucker used a pay phone to call police.[214]

Irvin said, "Any man in his right mind don't want to be kept locked up, but I'm going to be truthful with you. In a way, I'm sort of glad it's all over." Irvin said his final decision to escape was driven by the fact that he believed Indiana authorities "were never going to get me a new trial....So I wrote a letter to my lawyer and told him I was leaving." Irvin said he fled to California because "I like the weather."[215]

Gibson County sheriff Earl Hollen escorted Irvin back to Indiana by holding him on the end of a chain resembling a dog leash. The continued "chaining" of Irvin quickly earned him the name "Mad Dog" among newspaper reporters.

Irvin was convicted in Gibson County of the December 23, 1954 murder of an Evansville gas station attendant, Wesley Kerr, twenty-nine. His case had been moved from Vanderburgh County on a change of venue. He was also implicated in five other murders: the December 2, 1954 slaying of Mary Holland, thirty-three; the March 21, 1955 murder of Wilhelmina Sailer, forty-seven; and the triple murder of Goebel Duncan, fifty-one, his son, Raymond Duncan, twenty-nine, and Elizabeth Duncan, twenty, Goebel's daughter-in-law, all on March 28, 1955, in Henderson, Kentucky.

In August 1956, the Indiana Supreme Court entered a stay of execution for Irvin in the Kerr murder to allow his attorneys to pursue an appeal based on the claim that he was convicted in a court atmosphere of bias. On July 9, 1957, the U.S. Court of Appeals granted Irvin an indefinite stay of execution, just hours before he was to be executed.

On November 9, 1960, the U.S. Supreme Court heard oral arguments in Washington, D.C., regarding Irvin's claims that his Sixth Amendment rights had been violated. The nation's highest court overruled Irvin's conviction for the Kerr murder on June 5, 1961—the first time the nation's high court has ever overturned a murder conviction based on pretrial publicity surrounding the case.

Supreme Court justice Tom Clark wrote, "With his life at stake, it is not requiring too much that [Irvin] be tried in an atmosphere undisturbed by so huge a wave of public passion and by a jury in which two-thirds of the members admit, before hearing any testimony, to possessing a belief in his guilt."[216]

Irvin was tried again, this time outside of Gibson County in Sullivan County. He was convicted again of the Kerr murder on June 13, 1962. He received a life sentence to be served at the Indiana State Prison. He remained there until his death from lung cancer on November 9, 1983.

THE HUMAN FLY PROVES AN ELUSIVE, VIOLENT OUTLAW

Fugitive(s): Ivan L. Deckard

Wanted For: June 24, 1958, escape, Indiana Reformatory, Pendleton, Indiana

April 13, 1959, escape, U.S. Courthouse, St. Louis, Missouri

Captured: October 3, 1958, St. Louis, Missouri

May 17, 1959, University City, Missouri

Ivan L. Deckard earned the unofficial title of the "human fly" after a dramatic escape from the U.S. Federal Courthouse in downtown St. Louis on April 13, 1959.

It was just his latest "accomplishment" in the growing list of criminal exploits of the Indiana fugitive who had been captured as an escapee from the Indiana Reformatory when arrested in St. Louis. Deckard's latest foray into criminal activity appeared to be one that included stepping up the violence.

When he was arrested at the Roosevelt Hotel in downtown St. Louis on October 3, 1958, police reported they found a submachine gun and a revolver in his hotel room and said Deckard, thirty, had plans to rob a bank. Detectives were looking for him in the first place on warrants charging him with passing about $10,000 in worthless checks around the city since June.[217]

Apparently unconcerned about how the police would deal with him, once in custody, he listed his occupation as "forger." It was an apt title. Seized from Deckard's hotel room were eighty payroll checks issued by the Hancock Trucking Company stolen from its offices in a burglary, as well as a check-writing machine and other office equipment needed to create phony checks.

Deckard openly admitted that he was a fugitive from Indiana, where he had served only three years of a thirty-three-year sentence given to him for arson and forgery. He detailed a series of street holdups he said he conducted in Chicago and other cities, always making sure to take the person's identification to use later as part of his bogus check passing schemes. Deckard said his future plans included going to San Francisco "to pull a big job."[218]

Check passing had been Deckard's profession for most of his adult life. Originally arrested in Bedford and Bloomington on related charges, the Heltonville native was also suspected of forging checks in the Vincennes area. A father of four children, his biggest conviction came on five counts of arson for a March 12, 1957 fire that destroyed the Shields Grocery store in rural Monroe County. A Monroe County grand jury found that Deckard had made a deal with Earl Shields, the operator of the grocery, three days before the massive blaze to burn the store to collect insurance proceeds.[219]

It is unclear why Deckard chose to escape the Pendleton reformatory in June 1958, as he was eligible for at least a consideration of parole two months later in August. Regardless, he and Howard A. Crook, twenty-nine, absconded with the car of a prison employee and drove away unmolested.[220]

Deckard remained at large until his penchant for criminal activity over honest work caught up with him in St. Louis. His reputation, however, was not yet complete. Held in a courthouse cell moments after completing a hearing in the federal courtroom of Judge George H. Moore, Deckard took out a concealed hacksaw and removed the bars from a holding cell adjacent to the courtroom.

"Deckard used a one-foot hacksaw blade to saw a bar in a window of the cell, which is on the third floor [of the courthouse]," the *St. Louis Post-Dispatch* reported. "He then lowered himself to a second-floor window by means of an electric cord. There he entered a window in the office of the Internal Revenue Service, and then made his way to the ground floor."[221]

Once outside the courthouse, Deckard successfully commandeered a 1½-ton truck and sped away. IRS employees, obviously curious about a large, six-foot-three man who had climbed into the window of their office, telephoned the court above them and asked if they were missing a prisoner. It wasn't until then that Deckard's escape was discovered.

Hours after fleeing the courthouse, Deckard attempted to rob a drugstore in the western suburb of St. Louis known as University City. He entered the Irwin Drug Store at 6601 Olive Boulevard, brandishing a gun and concealing his face with a handkerchief. "This is a holdup," Deckard warned the store employees and patrons. "Make a false move, and I'll kill all of you."[222]

Unknown to Deckard, however, as he entered the drugstore, the store's owner was on a pay phone inside a booth in the store talking to his girlfriend. He told her to call the police immediately to report the robbery in progress. Two University City patrolmen, Raymond Bruno and Stanley Topper, quickly arrived.

In the short time Deckard had been away from the federal courthouse, he had somehow obtained a .38-caliber handgun and, in no short order, used it to engage officers Bruno and Topper in a violent gun battle outside the store. Likely aiding Deckard in obtaining the gun was an old friend he had picked up to help in the robbery, a thirty-four-year-old ex-con named Herbert John Lorts. In the shootout, Lorts was fatally wounded, while both officers and Deckard also suffered gunshot wounds but were not seriously injured.

After robbing the store and losing his partner Lorts in the shootout, Deckard made multiple stops. First, he stopped and entered the home of Mrs. Oliver Fisher Sr., whom he ordered at gunpoint to bandage his bullet-wounded arm and give him a clean shirt. He then decided to take with him as a hostage, twenty-three-year-old Richard Wetzel, who was visiting the Fischer home at the time. He later released Wetzel uninjured and then made his way to the home of Curtis Link, another ex-con friend, and his young wife, Jeannine, who lived about four blocks from the drugstore. As police surrounded the apartment building where Curtis and Jeannine Link lived (with Mrs. Link clutching her newborn baby as she was taken by police), officers made their way to the attic of the building. Their hunch that Deckard was hiding there was correct, as officers said he cried out, "Don't shoot, I'm coming down," as they went up the attic stairs. In the attic, the officers found an unloaded snub-nosed revolver. As he was led from the scene in handcuffs, he gloated to bystanders and a newspaper photographer, "I'm not yellow, I just ran out of ammunition."[223]

THE TEEN ESCAPE ARTIST

Fugitive(s): Carl Reiselt
Wanted For: February 18, 1959, escape, Indiana Reformatory, Pendleton, Indiana
February 19, 1959, burglary, kidnapping, Tuscola, Illinois
Captured: February 19, 1959, Decatur, Illinois

Although he was only eighteen years old, Carl Reiselt won the begrudging respect of law enforcement officials across two states after escaping the Indiana Reformatory at Pendleton on February 18, 1959, by hiding inside a rail car.

It wasn't Reiselt's first jail escape, but it certainly was his most daring. After he was captured, prison and police officials referred to him as an "escape artist" and "an accomplished fugitive." The evidence shows that although he was still a teenager, he was as bold as any veteran criminal many years older.

Associated Press writers seemed impressed with the youth's exploits, moving a story with the dramatic lead: "A teen-age prisoner escaped and disarmed and kidnapped a policeman, terrorized a couple in their home, and took two hostages on a wild flight that ended in his capture by a determined sheriff."[224]

Reiselt benefited from not being discovered as missing by prison officials for several hours. Reiselt was fleeing from a ten-year burglary sentence given to him by a Montgomery County judge. Once outside the reformatory, police said Reiselt broke into a Pendleton-area home, switched out of his prison garb for clothes he found in the house and stole the family's car.

From there, he drove west into Illinois, stopping around Midnight at Tuscola, Illinois, a county seat town about 165 miles west of Pendleton. In Tuscola, he broke into Todd's Hardware Store in the downtown district, where he stole a .22-caliber pistol and ammunition. "But in climbing through a broken window, Reiselt cut a four-inch gash in his head," the *Decatur Daily Review* reported.[225]

Once armed, Reiselt selected the William Nisbet home in Tuscola at random and found a widow, Mrs. Carolyn Timmons, and her friend Jack Brown watching television. "Confronting them with the pistol, Reiselt ordered Brown to take him to a doctor" for treatment of his wound. "As Reiselt forced Brown into Brown's car, the Nisbet family telephoned police and the sheriff for help." Moments later, Tuscola police patrol officer Raymond Prosser arrived at the home of Dr. William Steiner, a local physician, whom Reiselt planned to force him to treat his wound. "When Reiselt saw the squad car, he threatened Brown with the pistol and forced him into the car with Officer Prosser," the *Decatur Daily Review* reported. "Prosser was unable to counter the move for fear Brown would be shot."[226]

Douglas County sheriff Eugene Miller, who also responded to the Nisbet family's call for help, came to the physician's home but encountered a desperate Reiselt, who told the sheriff he would kill the officer and Brown if he approached. "Telling his two captives that he was headed for Missouri, Reiselt forced Prosser to drive about 60 miles an hour out Route 36 toward Decatur, Illinois," newspaper accounts told. "Reiselt occupied the rear seat, covering the two men in the front seat." Two miles west of Tuscola, he released Brown from the squad car and kept only the police officer as a hostage. "Sheriff Miller trailed the car for 38 miles to Decatur with his headlights turned off, apparently without Reiselt's knowledge."[227]

Becoming confused about his directions once in Decatur, Reiselt ordered Prosser to make a U-turn, allowing Sheriff Miller to block the car and get the jump on Reiselt. Once in custody, his amazing escape odyssey complete, Rieselt was taken to a local hospital for treatment of his head wound and returned to jail.

A TWO-FOR-ONE CAPTURE FOR THE FBI

Fugitive(s): Ernest Tait and Raymond "Red" Duvall
Wanted For: Tait, December 1958, burglary, bail skipping, Crawfordsville, Indiana
Duvall, July 29, 1959, escape, State Prison, Michigan City, Indiana
Captured: September 10, 1960, Denver, Colorado

The old adage that "there's strength in numbers" didn't hold true for Hoosier fugitives Ernest Tait and Raymond "Red" Duvall, as both were snatched up by FBI agents on a downtown street in Denver, Colorado, on September 10, 1960.

While FBI agents were officially looking for "trigger happy" Tait, they lucked out to find him in the company of Duvall, also wanted in Indiana. Tait was the big prize, officially on the FBI's Ten Most Wanted list, but the FBI was happy to arrest both men and return them to Indiana.[228]

News reports indicated that Tait, forty-nine, was apprehended before he could get to his car nearby, where a .38-caliber revolver was found lying on the front seat, wrapped in a newspaper. Tait, placed on the top ten list in June 1960, was wanted for skipping his bail just before his April 1959 trial in Montgomery County for the December 1958 burglary of a Crawfordsville bottling plant.

Duvall, fifty-two, was a notorious convicted murderer from Indianapolis who had walked away from the Indiana State Prison on July 29, 1959. At the time of his escape, Duvall was assigned to a prison garage as a mechanic based on his trustee status.[229]

"It happened so fast, we didn't have a chance to speak," Tait told a reporter about the swiftness with which the FBI nabbed the two men.[230]

As the *Indianapolis Star* reported, Tait was a prized catch for the FBI. He was on the agency's famed top ten list for the second time (a rare achievement for *any* criminal) and had been traced to the Denver area. "It was believed he was armed with a submachine gun, but none was in his possession when he was caught," the *Star* reported. "The Hoosier outlaw had vowed he would never be taken alive."[231]

The FBI bulletin issued for Tait in June 1960 described him as "a trigger-happy, veteran outlaw" and "a chronic criminal." The feds also said Tait had been "convicted previously of unlawfully obtaining explosives and burglary" and was "an avid gambler who is fond of horse racing, auto racing and prize fights. Tait is reportedly armed with a submachine gun, has been known to be armed with a .45 caliber automatic pistol and has engaged police officers in gun battles. He should be considered extremely dangerous."[232]

Once in custody, Tait didn't fight extradition and was returned to Crawfordsville to face trial on his original charges related to the burglary. An April 1961 trial was conducted, and Tait was convicted in less than two hours on charges of breaking and entering to commit a felony.[233]

Interestingly, despite Tait's previous history of bail jumping, Special Judge Paul D. Ewan gave him a $10,000 cash bond while he appealed his conviction.[234] True to his past, Tait again skipped bond and failed to appear for scheduled court hearings on his appeal in July 1963. Police in Van Nuys, California, finally caught up with Tait in September 1963 and returned him to Indiana, where he was ordered to immediately begin serving a one- to ten-year sentence (which he had been appealing).[235]

For Tait, it was the end of a lifetime of crime in Indiana. He was first arrested at age nineteen as the "companion of a girl bandit" in an Indianapolis robbery in February 1930, as police said Tait drove a getaway car for a young woman who held up two men on Kentucky Avenue. Five years later, Tait made major headlines in Indianapolis for the January 25, 1935 holdup of the Speedway State Bank, which ended in a shootout. "His arms and legs filled with buckshot and with two rifle bullet holes in his body," the twenty-year-old Tait was arrested in his home, where he was declining rapidly, having forgone receiving any medical treatment for his injuries for fear of being arrested.

Eventually convicted, Tait was sentenced to ten years in prison at Michigan City but began the first of several elusive moves in July 1936, just eight months into his sentence. Prison officials were red-faced that Tait had escaped as he worked as part of a gang repairing an exterior wall to the prison.

Tait remained elusive. Indianapolis police came close to capturing him in April 1938, engaging in a car chase through the city with shots being fired in both directions. "A slim young man with Dillinger-like skill at a steering wheel continued to evade capture today over west side streets that would have been the envy of Hollywood," the *Indianapolis News* reported.[236] Police said they learned of Tait's presence in the city after a tip was called in that he was attending a West Washington Street carnival seeking help in getting tattoos removed from his arms.

Tait's luck finally ran out in October 1938, when he was arrested in Chicago. "Tait was captured in a hand-to-hand fight with postal inspectors and state's attorney police in a Chicago saloon," an *Indianapolis News* account relayed. At his arrest, Tait "showed off scars of his machine gun bullet wounds in an outburst of boasting."[237]

As spectacular as Tait's record of escape and eluding the police was, his Hoosier counterpart arrested with him on the Denver street corner in September 1960, Raymond Duvall, was an equally remarkable criminal figure. Duvall was one of two men convicted for the brazen March 1937 robbery and murder of seventy-four-year-old Indianapolis businessman Clayton J. Potts.

The robbery of Potts had been bold—a midday take of more than $2,500 in payroll funds the elderly foundry owner was about to pay out to his employees. "After shooting Potts, the gunman ran from the company office, joined a companion waiting in an automobile, and escaped after a wild chase through downtown streets and into the south side that ended with the abandonment of the bandit automobile," the *Indianapolis News* reported.[238]

Police quickly identified Duvall and another known fugitive, Leonard Jackson, as the two men wanted in the robbery. Months of searching, however, proved fruitless. "Over a trail marked by murder and desperate gun battles, Midwest authorities spent today in a widespread search for two former Indiana convicts," the *Indianapolis News* relayed.[239]

The end of Duvall's fugitive run finally came on January 21, 1939, when he was arrested while sleeping in an abandoned farmhouse near Alexandria, Louisiana. FBI agents joined in the surprise arrest of Duvall, who was also a suspect in a nearly $40,000 robbery of a bank at Charleston, West Virginia. Officers said Duvall offered no resistance, uttering only, "You've got me, so what's the use of talking?"[240]

He was returned to Indianapolis to face murder and robbery charges, and Duvall's case was eventually transferred to Shelby County, where he was convicted in June 1939 and sentenced to life in prison. He was serving that life sentence when he escaped the state prison in July 1959.

Twenty-four inmates took Independence Day literally on July 4, 1920, and slipped out of the Marion County Jail in Indianapolis while the sheriff slept. *The Indiana Album.*

South Bend robbery and murder suspect Thomas O'Brien escaped the Elkhart County Jail at Goshen on September 16, 1926. *Goshen Historical Society.*

Knox County sheriff Abe J. Westfall (*center*) with deputies at the Vincennes jail, who couldn't hold cop killer Dreyfus Rhodes in 1927. *Knox County Public Library, Norbert Brown Collection.*

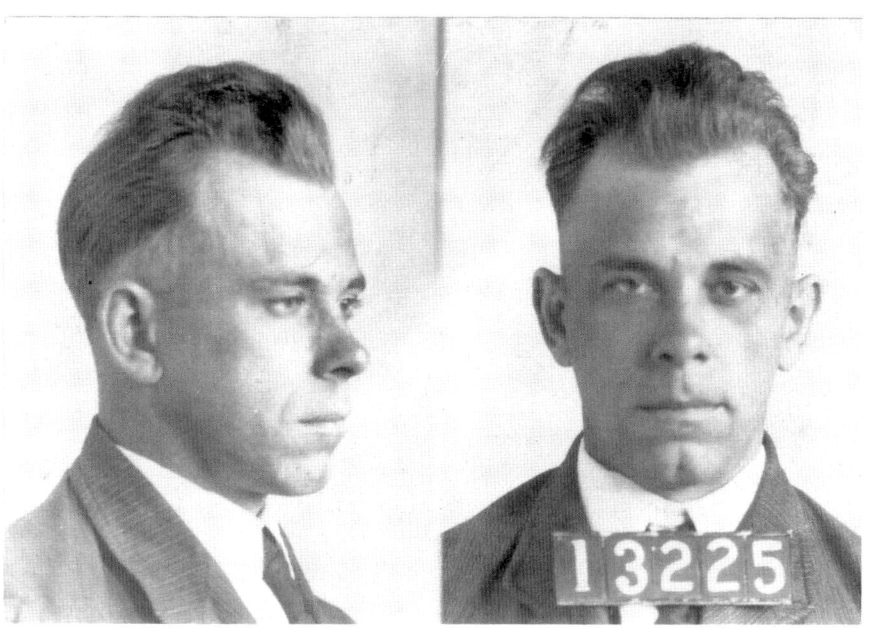

Indiana's most infamous fugitive of all time, John Dillinger. *The Indiana Album.*

Hoosier fugitive John Dillinger awaits a hearing in a Crown Point courtroom. *The Indiana Album.*

The Indianapolis Interurban Bus garage, servicing the new buses (*left*) was commandeered by robbers in February 1933, leaving a city police officer dead. *The Indiana Album.*

WANTED

JOHN HERBERT DILLINGER

On June 23, 1934, HOMER S. CUMMINGS, Attorney General of the United States, under the authority vested in him by an Act of Congress approved June 6, 1934, offered a reward of

$10,000.00

for the capture of John Herbert Dillinger or a reward of

$5,000.00

for information leading to the arrest of John Herbert Dillinger.

DESCRIPTION

Age, 32 years; Height, 5 feet 7-1/8 inches; Weight, 153 pounds; Build, medium; Hair, medium chestnut; Eyes, grey; Complexion, medium; Occupation, machinist; Marks and scars, 1/2 inch scar back left hand, scar middle upper lip, brown mole between eyebrows.

All claims to any of the aforesaid rewards and all questions and disputes that may arise as among claimants to the foregoing rewards shall be passed upon by the Attorney General and his decisions shall be final and conclusive. The right is reserved to divide and allocate portions of any of said rewards as between several claimants. No part of the aforesaid rewards shall be paid to any official or employee of the Department of Justice.

If you are in possession of any information concerning the whereabouts of John Herbert Dillinger, communicate immediately by telephone or telegraph collect to the nearest office of the Division of Investigation, United States Department of Justice, the local addresses of which are set forth on the reverse side of this notice.

JOHN EDGAR HOOVER, DIRECTOR,
DIVISION OF INVESTIGATION,
UNITED STATES DEPARTMENT OF JUSTICE,
WASHINGTON, D. C.

June 25, 1934

Left: Wanted poster for John Dillinger. *FBI.gov.*

Below: "Wee Willie" Mason slipped out of the Hamilton County Jail at Noblesville on August 21, 1934. *Steve Polston.*

"Wee Willie" Mason was eventually captured by police but not before losing a leg in a shootout with police, shown here entering the Hamilton County Courthouse in November 1934. *Indianapolis News.*

In the aftermath of the Dillinger fugitive era, a bullet-proof police booth was constructed on the courthouse square in Goshen. Here, local and state police show off their preparedness for any would-be fugitives. *Goshen Historical Society.*

Witnesses lineup outside the Nevada state "death house" at Carson City for the September 29, 1944 execution of seventeen-year-old Floyd Loveless. *Janice Oberding.*

Right: Floyd Loveless stands for a Nevada lineup in 1942. *Janice Oberding.*

Below: Tippecanoe County youth Floyd Loveless after his arrest by Nevada authorities for killing a police officer. *Janice Oberding.*

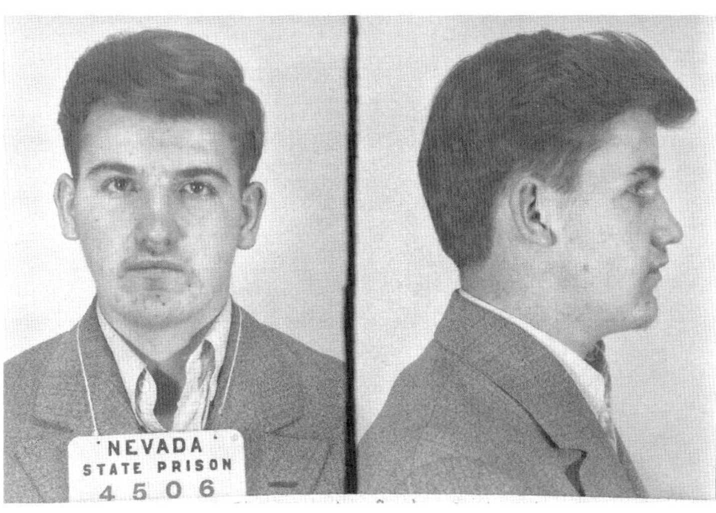

Accused Evansville serial killer Leslie "Mad Dog" Irvin poses for news photographers while under arrest by San Francisco police in February 1956. *Author collection.*

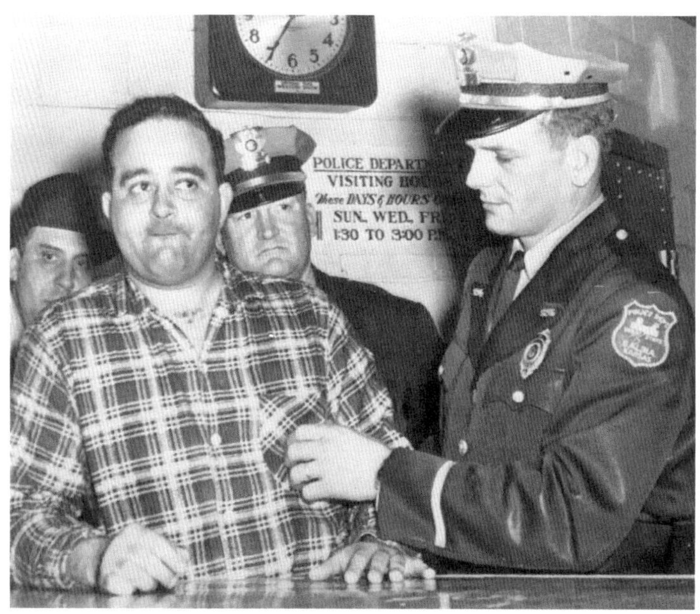

Escaped mental patient Watson Young Jr. under arrest in Salina, Kansas, in February 1962, following a brutal double murder and rape in Indianapolis in December 1961. *Author collection.*

Edith Louise Schmidt at her April 1967 trial in Jay County for the murder and dismemberment of her estranged husband. *Jerry Miller.*

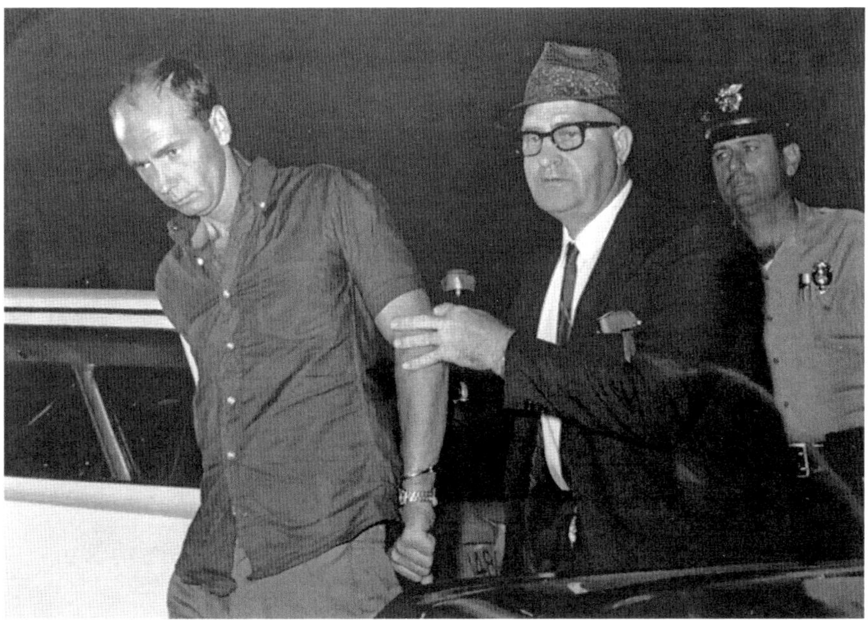

Indiana fugitive Arthur C. Murray is escorted by police in Lincoln, Nebraska, after an August 1967 deadly shootout that left a police detective dead. *Author collection.*

Lincoln, Nebraska police escort Howard Crooks, an Indiana State Prison escapee, for his role in an August 1967 shootout. *Author collection.*

The former Indiana Women's Prison in Indianapolis lost three inmates between 1969 and 1972. One female fugitive remained at large for more than twenty years before being recaptured. *Steve Polston.*

WANTED BY THE FBI

ESCAPED FEDERAL PRISONER; RACKETEER-INFLUENCED AND CORRUPT ORGANIZATIONS - MURDER, ARSON; MAIL FRAUD; CONSPIRACY

MICHAEL GEORGE THEVIS

DESCRIPTION

Born February 25, 1932, Raleigh, North Carolina (not supported by birth records); Height, 5'10"; Weight, 170 to 175 pounds; Build, medium; Hair, brown - balding; Eyes, brown; Complexion, medium; Race, white; Nationality, American; Occupations, corporation president, newsstand operator, publisher, restaurant operator; Scars and Marks, scars on right temple, left side of nose, under chin and both legs, two joints of right ring finger amputated; Remarks, may walk with limp, wear brace on left leg and use cane due to hip disorder, may be clean shaven, known to spend excessively; Social Security Number used, 266-40-2390.

CRIMINAL RECORD

Thevis has been convicted of interstate transportation of obscene matter and conspiracy to commit arson.

CAUTION

THEVIS, A NATIONALLY KNOWN DISTRIBUTOR OF PORNOGRAPHY, IS BEING SOUGHT AS AN ESCAPEE FROM CUSTODY AND FOR HIS ALLEGED PARTICIPATION IN TWO MURDERS AND FOUR ATTEMPTS TO KILL GOVERNMENT WITNESSES. BECAUSE THEVIS HAS USED FIREARMS AND EXPLOSIVE DEVICES IN THE PAST, HE SHOULD BE CONSIDERED ARMED, DANGEROUS, AND AN ESCAPE RISK.

Left: Michael Thevis, the self-proclaimed "King of Porn," escaped the Floyd County Jail in New Albany in 1978 and later ordered a double murder. *FBI.gov.*

Below: Though an imposing structure when it first opened in 1860, the Indiana State Prison at Michigan City has struggled to hold on to some of its charges over the decades. *Public domain.*

The main entrance to the Indiana State Prison at Michigan City circa 1904.

5

1960–69

A SHORT STINT ON THE TOP TEN LIST

Fugitive(s): Edward Reiley
Wanted For: December 4, 1959, bank robbery, Hamlet, Indiana
January 29, 1960, bank robbery, Logansport, Indiana
Captured: May 24, 1960, Rockford, Illinois

Edward Reiley had the distinction of being on the FBI's Ten Most Wanted list for all of twenty-four-hours after an alert car salesman in Bradley, Illinois, recognized his picture from a wanted notice printed in a local newspaper.

The FBI was well into its practice of identifying its most-wanted fugitives by the spring of 1960, and the tactic was working. In fact, FBI officials gloated to Sam Fogg, a United Press International correspondent in Washington, D.C., that Reiley had been captured by the same tried-and-true method that had ended the run of more famous fugitives, such as Billy the Kid, Jesse James and John Dillinger.

FBI officials told reporters that Reiley's arrest "was just the most recent instance in which wanted posters such as those familiar to post office walls proved the downfall of a criminal. The FBI unhesitatingly credits scores of arrests to the circulars and to a sharp-eye public. Since April 1959, approximately 150 fugitives have been apprehended, 45 percent of them picked up as a direct result of wanted posters."[241]

Reiley was wanted for two Indiana bank robberies, the first coming in the tiny Starke County community of Hamlet on December 4, 1959. Netting only $3,990 in cash, Reiley held bank employees at gunpoint for about five minutes and ordered them to remain inside an inner office in the bank for ten minutes. He apparently believed a bank manager's bluff that the bank's safe had a time-delayed combination and fled with what he could get.

Reiley was identified in the case by a sundries shop proprietor who looked out her store window and saw him fleeing in a 1956 white Chevrolet just after removing a mask over his face. The witness, an elderly woman named Mary Wright, was sharp-eyed, reporting the car's license plate and direction of travel as well.[242]

Remaining at large, Reiley popped up again sixty miles directly south in Logansport, Indiana, where he held up the Eastgate Shopping Center branch of the Farmers and Merchants Bank on January 29, 1960. His second attempt was more successful, netting him just under $20,000 in cash. As was the case in the Hamlet robbery, Reiley "commandeered" the bank and its employees by leaping over a counter and pointing a loaded weapon in their faces. As he had in the earlier stick-up, he ordered his loot placed in a pillowcase.

Interestingly, in the Logansport robbery, Reiley did not bother to cover his face. Bank vice-president Charles Kingery reported that the man approached his desk in the bank calmly. "I saw this man coming in and I started to walk toward him and he said, 'I know you, Mr. Kingery.'…Then he pulled the gun and jumped over my desk and ordered me to start walking toward the vault. I don't remember ever having seen the man before."[243]

Reiley apparently had done his research. He warned bank employees to not call police. Kingery said he remarked, "I am going to say this once. I know you [Mr. Kingery] and I know where you live. I know that you drive a white Thunderbird." Reiley also pointed to one of the tellers and said, "I know you too, and I know where you live." Kingery said, "He ordered us to remain in the rest room for 10 minutes or that his brother would shoot us. He went outside and told us to lock the door from the inside and that he would shoot through the door if he didn't hear the door locked. We waited about eight minutes and came out and phoned the police."[244]

Within thirty minutes of the robbery, the Indiana State Police had established a roadblock thirty miles northwest of Logansport, at Buffalo, a White County community on the Tippecanoe River. There, Indiana State Police encountered a fleeing Reiley, who attempted to blow their roadblock but not before striking an Indiana State Police car driven by Lieutenant Erwin J. Rhoda. Rhoda reportedly fired several shots at Reiley's car.

The bullet holes in Reiley's car were his ultimate downfall. Making it as far west as Bradley, Illinois (about ninety miles northwest of White and Cass Counties), Reiley went to a car dealer in Rockford, Illinois, looking for a replacement vehicle. While he was able to make a trade, the car dealer remained curious (because of the bullet holes and blown out back window of the car Reiley traded in) and later recognized him from newspaper accounts of his exploits.

As police closed in on Reiley, they briefly held his wife, Shirley Reiley, a Hobart, Indiana mother of five, who in the days after the Logansport bank robbery paid for a new home with twenty-eight $100 bills, raising suspicions. The FBI later confirmed a portion of the funds she used were from the bank robberies (based on serial numbers on the bills) but cleared Mrs. Reiley of any wrongdoing.[245]

A federal jury at South Bend convicted Reiley on two counts of armed robbery in July 1960. U.S. District judge Robert A. Grant sentenced Reiley to a term of twenty years in federal prison for the two robberies on August 17, 1960. During the sentencing hearing, Judge Grant took the unusual tact of asking Reiley what he had done with the money he stole—most of which was never recovered. "I don't know," Reiley told the judge. "It was gone three days after I got it. I used the Logansport money and some of my own to pay off a 12-year debt." The judge asked to whom the money was paid, and Reiley refused to reply.[246]

MURDEROUS MENTAL PATIENT AND FUGITIVE

Fugitive(s): Watson Young Jr.
Wanted For: March 1961, escape, Central State Mental Hospital, Louisville, Kentucky
December 13, 1961, double murder and rape, Indianapolis, Indiana
Captured: February 12, 1962, Salina, Kansas

The February 12, 1962 dramatic capture of escaped mental hospital patient and murder fugitive Watson Young Jr. was the stuff frightening movies and crime novels are made of.

Wanted for the murder of an Indianapolis couple who had tried to help him and the rape of an Indiana woman, Young, thirty-one, stole an ambulance and led Salina, Kansas authorities on a wild chase before finally being captured by authorities.

The *Salina Journal* reported, "His arrest about Midnight Monday climaxed a hair-raising police chase of a siren-screaming ambulance stolen from the Rush Smith Funeral Home." Salina police patrol officers saw the ambulance being driven at a high rate of speed before it was even reported as stolen. Police said the ambulance was traveling as fast as ninety miles per hour on a city street, its siren whaling. When they stopped him near the entrance to St. John's Military School, police questioned the driver, Young, who lied and said he was en route to help deliver a baby.

He later told an officer, "If you don't kill me, I'll tell you who I am. I'm Watson Young and I'm wanted by the FBI for murder." Young took from his pocket a copy of the FBI wanted poster bearing his image. The FBI bulletin about Young described him as "a schizophrenic paranoid," indicating "he suffers from alternate delusions of grandeur and persecution."[247]

On the day he was apprehended, Young had been on the FBI's Ten Most Wanted fugitives list for only eight days, based on the brutal December 13, 1961 slaying of Hansel E. Gupton, sixty-four, and his wife, Mary Alice, fifty-eight, in their home at 1524 East Seventeenth Street in Indianapolis.

After fatally shooting the Guptons, who had befriended him and offered him a place to stay in their home, Young "tricked his way" into the nearby home of a twenty-two-year-old "housewife" who was caring for her child and raped and beat her. Unknown to the Guptons and his rape victim was the troubling fact that Young was at the time a walk away escapee from Central State Hospital, a mental institution located near Louisville, Kentucky. He had been missing from the hospital for nine months when he surfaced in Indianapolis. Police in Louisville and Evansville were also seeking Young for passing a set of bad checks there.[248]

Young had been given a place to stay for a brief time by the Guptons, who were known to help others in their neighborhood. In fact, one neighborhood girl who had gone to the Gupton home the afternoon of the murder to see if Mrs. Gupton would give her a bowl of peaches and cream (something she was known to do for neighborhood children), was turned away by a gruff Young, who met her at the front door. She was unharmed.

Inside the Gupton home, "Mrs. Gupton's body was found on the kitchen floor of her home about 3:55 p.m. by her daughter-in-law," the *Indianapolis Star* reported. "She had been shot behind the right ear. The body of Hansel Gupton was found in the basement more than a half hour later when police finally searched the home.[249]

As Indianapolis police were investigating the Gupton murder, a new report came of an unconscious woman less than a mile away in a home in the 2100 block of Brookside Parkway. There, police found the young mother unconscious and the victim of a rape and beating. "Both the rape victim and her two-year-old daughter were choked by the intruder, a Negro, who told the terror-stricken woman, 'I'm a maniac,'" the *Star* reported.[250]

The victim, who regained consciousness, said Young came to her door and claimed his car had broken down and he wanted to call a taxi. She let the man in, and he then also asked to use the bathroom. "He came out of the bathroom with a knife in one hand and a razor in the other," a police detective told the *Star*. "The man was described as soft-spoken and polite, but changed his demeanor suddenly, ordering the woman and the little girl to disrobe. The young mother fought with him, but lost consciousness as he choked her. When she regained her senses, she found herself disrobed and saw the man coming from another room with the little girl who was also criminally assaulted." From descriptions given, police quickly linked the Gupton murder with the subsequent rape and beating. As a result, "The search for an escaped maniac spread from Lake Michigan to the Ohio River last night," the *Indianapolis Star* reported.[251]

Police said Young stole his rape victim's 1952 Ford but not before "binding her hands with tape and making her swear on a Bible she would not tell her husband [of the attack]." Many people did not take Young as any sort of violent threat. Dr. Walter Fox, superintendent of the state mental facility in Kentucky, said Young was under supervision as a result of his record of passing bad checks. Fox told a reporter that "he has a behavior problem, but he is not insane."[252]

The rather tame description of Young provided by Fox was at odds with what reporters uncovered after his despicable acts in Indianapolis. An *Indianapolis Star* report indicated that Young had been committed to state mental facilities in Kentucky at least three times before. "Psychiatrists who examined Young did not agree with the courts that he was insane," however. "None of the hospital records available indicated a medical filing of insanity."[253]

In December 1963, Young was found guilty of two counts of murder for the slaying of the Guptons, following a four-day trial in Hamilton County Circuit Court. Judge Charles W. Ardery Jr. sentenced Young to life in prison.[254]

A "GOOD KID" BECOMES A COLD-BLOODED KILLER

Fugitive(s): Gary D. Rardon
Wanted For: July 6, 1962, murder, Hamilton County, Indiana
November 1974, murders, Franklin Park and Prospect Heights, Illinois
Captured: December 8, 1962, New London, Connecticut
January 18, 1975, Louisville, Kentucky

On paper, all indications were that nineteen-year-old Gary Rardon was a good kid. The only son of United States Air Force recruiting sergeant William H. Rardon and his wife, he came from a well-heeled Northeast Indianapolis neighborhood and was a sailor in the U.S. Navy in 1962. His life was all downhill from there, though.

In July 1962, on leave from the navy and visiting his parents in Indianapolis, Rardon went out exploring and was hitchhiking along State Road 67 (Pendleton Pike) about two miles from his parent's home near Forty-Second and Post. The man who picked him up became Rardon's first victim of senseless violence.

The driver who stopped to pick up Rardon that day was twenty-three-year-old James Homer Smith, a traveling salesman for Arvin Industries, who was only four years older than Rardon. Smith had telephoned friends on July 6 and said he was en route from the Columbus area north to his father's home in Portland. "I'll see you in a couple of hours," Smith told a friend over the phone before setting off on his travels that day.[255]

It was the last time anyone talked to Smith, with his family, friends and coworkers growing more worried by the day.

Then, on July 11, about two miles outside of the town of Washington, Pennsylvania (just southwest of Pittsburgh), Smith's decomposing body was found by a farmer, dumped in a field. Although Smith's wallet and car were missing, police were able to identify him from a physical description given by family in Indiana, and the Portland High School class ring still on his finger. "The young man is believed to have died at least three or four days prior to being found," the *Columbus Evening Republican* reported.[256]

A coroner's inquest in Washington County, Pennsylvania, determined that Smith died of a single gunshot wound to the head. Smith had been shot with a .38-caliber weapon, the same type of weapon he was known to carry but was now missing.[257]

The mystery was how and why Smith's life ended more than three hundred miles east of his Indiana home. Although he was sometimes assigned by

Arvin to work in the Pittsburgh area, he was to be in Indiana at the time he went missing. Police reported that Smith was "known to have picked up hitchhikers and even to have allowed hitchhikers to drive his car while he slept. Mr. Smith may have been the victim of a hitchhiker....There have been no clues yet which can be used as a basis for determining what may have happened."[258]

Smith, who lived with his sister's family near Franklin, Indiana, was described as "a good employee" and "the driving member of the team" of three Arvin employees who sold and distributed exhaust systems. He had been employed by Arvin for just under a year when he went missing and was "considered a good worker and a 'steady' sort of a person," the *Columbus Evening Republican* noted. "It was not suspected that he would have become involved in trouble of any kind."[259]

Police attempted to retrace Smith's steps from the time he left the Columbus area on July 6, driving his brand-new 1962 white Chevrolet convertible, but the probe into Smith's murder went cold for almost six months. Then in early December 1962, police in New London, Connecticut, notified Indiana authorities that they were holding a nineteen-year-old AWOL sailor—Gary Rardon—who was found driving Smith's car and had Smith's driver's license and vehicle registration in his possession. "The sailor will be questioned about the death of Smith," an FBI spokesman said. "A warrant has been issued for Rardon's arrest on a charge of vehicle taking, and he will be questioned following disposal of the AWOL charges by the U.S. Navy."[260]

While extradition papers were prepared to return Rardon to Indiana, detectives confirmed that the investigation so far seemed to indicate that Smith was killed in Indiana and his body was transported to Pennsylvania in the trunk of his own car before being dumped.

The *Hartford Courant* dispatched a reporter to New London, Connecticut, to assess Rardon, as the case was making headlines in three states. A Connecticut judge quickly approved the order to extradite Rardon to Indiana. As Rardon was photographed and fingerprinted by Connecticut authorities one last time before being released, he said, "I feel sorry for my parents."[261]

The *Courant* reported, "He was dressed in a clean, white shirt and dark pants for his court appearance. The blond, clean-shaven youth appeared concerned but not upset by his arrest. He smiled occasionally and conversed quietly with police. Once, during the photographing, he asked the photographer, 'Should I scar my face to make me look like a hardened criminal?'"

The photographer replied, "Don't bother son, you're in enough trouble as is."[262]

Once in Indiana, authorities decided to file murder charges against Rardon in Hamilton County based on his statement to police that indicated the shooting occurred just over the Hamilton-Marion county line in Fall Creek Township. Eventually, Rardon decided to enter a guilty plea to a charge of voluntary manslaughter, avoiding a higher sentence for the charge of second-degree murder pending against him.

As he appeared in Hamilton Circuit Court on April 11, 1963, his parents were the only observers in the courtroom, and a reporter noted his mother wept throughout the hearing about the fate of her only child. Judge Charles Ardery briefly questioned Rardon as part of his decision about sentencing. "Rardon testified that he shot Smith after a struggle on a lonely county road north of Geist Reservoir," the *Noblesville Ledger* reported. "He said Smith asked him to take part in an improper sex act and that he got out of the car."[263]

"I was out 10 feet from the rear of the car when Smith got out with a gun in his hand," Rardon told the judge. "He ordered me back in the car. I walked toward him and when I got close enough, I grabbed for it. I got it away from him. Then he grabbed for it and I pulled the trigger."[264]

Accounts in the *Indianapolis Star* and the *Indianapolis News*, respectively, indicated that Rardon accused Smith of attempting to engage in "an unnatural act" or of making "an improper advance." Such an accusation came as a shock to most who knew Smith, a former star athlete in Jay County and ex-marine.[265] After Rardon killed Smith, he told the judge that "he tossed the motorist's body into the trunk of the car and then drove to Washington, Pennsylvania, where he dumped the body."[266]

Judge Ardery sentenced Rardon to a term of two to twenty-one years at the Indiana Reformatory in Pendleton. That is where Rardon remained until 1967, when he won parole, deemed by a prison psychiatrist to be rehabilitated and at little risk of further violence.[267]

Rardon served out his parole but eventually popped up again in a manner defying the assessment of the Indiana psychiatrist, who deemed him no further risk of violence. In January 1975, the FBI announced it had arrested Rardon in Louisville, Kentucky, on a fugitive warrant for two murders committed in the Chicago area. Rardon was the top suspect in the shotgun slayings of two Illinois residents during the course of robberies at Franklin Park and Prospect Heights in November 1974. At the time of the arrest, police said Rardon was in possession of a sawed-off twelve-gauge shotgun.[268]

Detectives determined that Rardon had relocated to the Chicago area from his parents' home in Indianapolis in 1974 after winning parole and was earning $250 a week as a machinist. It wasn't long before Rardon's presence in the Chicago area revealed that he was not clear of his tendency for violence.

On November 15, 1974, police in the Prospect Heights suburb of Chicago were trying to figure out who would want twenty-eight-year-old realtor Gene Ravenscraft dead. Ravenscraft's body was found in his Elmhurst Road office, a writing pen still in his hand. He had been killed by a shotgun blast to the face. No motive and no suspects were immediately identified.[269]

Police eventually linked witness statements and other evidence to Rardon and believed Ravenscraft was the victim of an attempted robbery. After he was under arrest by FBI agents in Louisville, Rardon provided "an initial confession" to Ravencraft's murder and was implicated in two other unsolved murders.[270]

On the same day Ravenscraft was slain, Asher Gruenberg, fifty, was found shot to death inside a Franklin Park garage office. He had also suffered a massive shotgun wound to the head. Gruenberg's credit cards and thirty dollars in cash were taken, police said, and the credit cards were traced to Rardon, being used in Indiana, Kentucky and Ohio.

Police eventually linked Rardon to a three-day crime spree that took not only the lives of Ravenscraft and Gruenberg but also a Hammond, Indiana cab driver named Herbert Noakes, thirty-one. Rardon's total take for the three murders was $161.

In February 1977, Rardon was sentenced to forty to one hundred years in the Illinois penal system. As he awaited sentencing, Rardon talked to *Chicago Tribune* reporter Jay Branegan in a rather matter-of-fact manner about the murders that had marked his life. "If a guy feels he can get away with the crime of blowing a person away, he'll do it no matter what the penalty," Rardon said. He said he was sorry for the murders he had committed: "I know that's not enough, but I'm sorry."[271]

Rardon was not eligible for the death penalty because it had been abolished in Illinois. Regardless, Rardon considered that might be the punishment he deserved. "This may sound funny, but I believe in the law. In one sense, I should [be executed] by legal standards." He was always a contradiction, though, saying that if he was given the death penalty, he would fight it. "It would take 15 guys to drag me to that thing. I wouldn't go with no goddamn dignity, I'll tell you that."[272]

Asked about his life, Rardon said he had been told he had an IQ of at least 117 when he was younger and possessed a strong competitive drive. As to why he had killed people during two different periods of his life, he could only add, "I may have a triple personality, instead of just a split one."[273]

Speaking specifically about the Illinois crime spree, Rardon said, "That whole two-week period I was in a daze. Each time I shot a person, all I got out of it was remorse. I couldn't even look at them after I shot them. What made me do it again and again, I don't know, it was like I couldn't control my actions, the actual pulling of the trigger." Asked about the second chance he had been given by Indiana authorities when they released him in 1967 for the Smith murder, Rardon said, "People say I fooled the psychiatrist to get out of prison in Indiana. That wasn't it at all. They just didn't see me in a depressed state of mind."[274]

Illinois officials considered Rardon for parole in 1987, a little over a decade into his new sentence for the shotgun murders. Cook County state attorney Richard Daley (later elected mayor of Chicago) said he opposed the release of Rardon, a "cold-blooded killer" who he deemed "too dangerous to ever be returned to society."[275] Rardon was eventually released on parole in October 2018 at the age of seventy-six.

A PREACHER'S SON GONE VERY BAD

Fugitive(s): Cozzie M. Jones
Wanted For: April 20, 1941, murder, West Terre Haute, Indiana
September 4, 1960, escape, Indiana State Prison, Michigan City, Indiana
March 24, 1961, murder, Tucson, Arizona
October 1962, murder, Joplin, Missouri
December 7, 1962, murder, Casa Grande, Arizona
Captured: December 7, 1962, Casa Grande, Arizona

Just six months before newspaper columns were overtaken by the entry of the United States into World War II in 1941, news accounts across the nation carried a troubling story of molest and murder from West Terre Haute, Indiana.

On April 21, 1941, police arrested Cozzie M. Jones, the twenty-four-year-old son of a Pentecostal minister in Vigo County, on a charge of murder. He was the only suspect in the drowning death of "church-going 12-year-old" Edith Idelle Barton.

"The girl's unclothed body was found in Sugar Creek near West Terre Haute early Monday," the Associated Press reported. "Cozzie Jones, only four months out of Pendleton State Reformatory [on parole], had admitted he had intimate relations with the girl near the creek Sunday night in an automobile belonging to his father, the Rev. C.M. Jones."[276] Jones, arrested as he walked along a road near the Wabash River just over the state line in Illinois, told police that he and the Barton girl had struggled in the car but that she had drown accidentally in the creek.

A signed statement from Jones said that he had made a clandestine "date" with the twelve-year-old girl, and the two scheduled to meet at 10:30 p.m. Barton was at the Jones home after attending Sunday services at Reverend Jones's church and was assisting in the care for an invalid sister of Cozzie Jones. She went home before dark but apparently had plans to return later to meet Cozzie.

"When Idelle came out to the garage," Jones said in his statement, "she had her nightgown on and was carrying a dress." He said the girl was a willing participant in his plans for a sexual encounter. The girl reportedly went willingly with Jones, who drove his father's car to a secluded area on the south edge of town, near a Sugar Creek bridge.[277]

Jones claimed that after his consensual sexual encounter with the young girl, she became upset and fled his car and later fell into the nearby creek and drowned. After he saw her dead body in the water, he said he went home and told his father what happened but did not notify police, "because the police would blame it on me." Jones, who had only been back at his parents' home since January, had been released early from a ten-year sentence he had previously been given for auto theft.[278]

The account Jones gave did not match up with the evidence, as police and a coroner found the girl nude in the water and with evidence of a beating. Drowning was not ruled out, but police were not convinced it was accidental.

The young girl's mother, identified in news accounts as Mrs. Mack Rogers, contradicted Cozzie's account that the girl had willingly come to his home in her nightgown. She said her daughter had gone to the Jones home earlier in the day to assist with the invalid girl and returned from Sunday services during the evening hours and then went to bed. "Some time later, Mrs. Rogers awakened and noticed the rear door [of her home] was open," the *Chicago Tribune* reported. "She went to the girl's room and found her clothing lying there and the bed covers thrown back, indicating the girl had been in the bed."[279]

Eventually, Jones was indicted on charges of rape and murder and was housed at the Vigo County Jail awaiting trial. In July 1941, guards successfully thwarted his attempt to saw his way out of the jail, and attempted escape charges were added.[280]

A trial for Jones was conducted in December 1941, less than a month after the Japanese attack on Pearl Harbor, and included twenty witnesses, including Jones himself. Jones denied killing the girl. He also told jurors he was addicted to morphine and barbiturates and was under the influence of "sleeping powder" when he signed a confession statement in the case.[281]

Jurors deliberated only thirty minutes before convicting Jones of second-degree murder. Vigo County judge John W. Gerdink sentenced Jones to a term of life in prison. That would have been the end of matters, but Jones decided otherwise almost two decades later, and on September 4, 1960, he walked away from the Summit Prison Farm in LaPorte County.[282]

Jones's whereabouts remained unknown for two years, until police in Arizona picked him up in December 1962 for questioning in at least two new murders. Under intense police interrogation, Jones once again readily gave up details of his alleged crimes. In addition, while police investigated the December 1962 murder of a Tucson man, they quickly gained interest in talking to Jones about the unsolved March 24, 1961 disappearance and murder of eight-year-old Marguerita A. Bejarano, who lived around the corner from Jones in a quiet, poor Tucson neighborhood. Marguerita was last seen as she was walking from home to Roosevelt Elementary School. She never made it to school.

As the *Arizona Daily Star* reported, "The route taken by the girl goes through a semi-industrial district and for a two-block stretch is bordered by trash strewn desert. Several junk yards line the street." Her distraught mother reported the girl was an obedient child: "She is a very good little girl. She never goes anywhere without telling us."[283]

The search for "pretty, brown-haired" Marguerita came to a sad close on March 28, 1961, when a local man, thirty-four-year-old Clyde Noline, reported he had discovered her body in a sewage culvert while searching for a drink of water in the hot Arizona sun. She had been shot twice in the head.[284]

"The body of the pretty child, her clothing pulled up over her head, was found in a desolate clump of tumbleweed and brush under a bridge carrying the Casa Grande Highway over Canada del Oro," the *Tucson Daily Citizen* noted. A coroner said he retrieved two .22-caliber slugs from Marguerita's head and that she had been dead at least forty-eight hours. "[The coroner] said there were no injuries to indicate she was molested sexually."[285]

Convicted sexual molesters and even friends and members of the Bejarano family were questioned about Marguerita's abduction and death, but no arrests were forthcoming as 1961 gave way to 1962. The case remained cold until December 1962, when police began questioning Cozzie Jones, a fugitive from Indiana, and a prime suspect in the murder of a Tempe, Arizona rancher.

Jones confessed to police that he had killed Carl Quast, sixty-two, in the desert west of Casa Grande, Arizona, on December 7, 1962. Living under the alias "Donald Steven Palmer," Jones even led police to Quast's body. Jones encountered Quast as two other men chased Jones. The men were chasing Jones after witnessing him trying to drag a ten-year-old girl into his car near Fortieth and Buckeye Streets. The two citizens gave chase of Jones in his car, until he turned into a dead-end street about a block from Quast's home. They backed off after Jones fired a shot at their car.

"Jones apparently accosted Quast in his carport where the Tempe man was cleaning a rifle after a hunting trip," the *Arizona Republic* reported. Quast's mother-in-law said she noticed Jones approaching "but suspected nothing when Quast entered the kitchen with the man, got the keys to his wife's car, and left hurriedly."[286]

Talking to a reporter from the *Phoenix Gazette* while in custody, Jones put the blame for Quast's murder on the victim: "He tried to hit me with a hammer. What could I do? Get wrecked and hurt me, too? That old man would still be alive if he hadn't tried to hit me with a hammer. He was a nice old guy. He talked nice to me."[287]

In addition to openly admitting he killed Quast, Jones revealed that he also killed a Nova Scotia man, Robert M. Fillmore, twenty-nine, in Joplin, Missouri, two months earlier in October 1962. Fillmore was described as a "psychic" traveling with a circus providing "readings" to save money to attend beautician school. "Authorities believe Fillmore was probably robbed and his car taken," the *Springfield News-Leader* reported in Missouri. "A motorist and his wife found Fillmore's body face down in a ditch on a country road west of Joplin. He had been shot twice in the back with a revolver."[288]

Tucson police were eager to talk to Jones, as his alias name of "Palmer" was on their suspect list. At the time of Marguerita Bejarano's murder, he lived just one block from the young girl. He was also arrested with a .22-caliber weapon, the same type used to kill the girl. Pima County sheriff Waldon V. Burr considered Jones a solid suspect. "Nearly all of his trouble has started with young girls," Burr said.[289]

On December 13, 1962, after questioning Jones, police charged him with Marguerita's murder, as well. Burr said Jones confessed after being told that ballistics tests were being made on his pistol to link him to the Bejarano case.

"The suspect has substantiated his confession in every important detail," Sheriff Burr said, including a reenactment of what he said happened on the day Marguerita died. While Jones was wanted for two other murders, Burr said he believed the other jurisdictions "may let Pima County have him due to the brutality, the age of the girl and the premeditation in the murder here. He might try to pull self-defense in the Tempe killing, but he can't do that here."[290]

In a signed statement to police, Jones said he woke on the morning of March 24, 1961, "with an urge to talk to a little girl." He said he drove around the neighborhood and saw Marguerita walking alone. "I caught up with her and asked her if she would like a ride to school, and she got into the car," Jones said. "She jumped right in, as happy as could be, but she began to argue when I turned past the school. She started crying as I passed the school and I drove to the freeway. I drove to the bridge and she was still crying and....I put my arms around her to try to comfort her. I asked her if she would tell on me. She said I was a nasty man and that she would tell her teacher, her mother and the police." Jones said he decided to shoot the girl after letting her get out of the car to get a drink of water from the nearby river. "I put her in some bushes and walked away, but I heard her groan, so I shot her again in the head."[291]

After murdering the girl and hiding her body, Jones said he sat in his car weeping for more than an hour but eventually returned to Tucson. He also confessed to having attended her funeral (along with many Tucson area residents) and "placed flowers on her grave every other day."[292]

Jones pleaded guilty to all charges on New Year's Eve 1962 and was sentenced to die in Arizona's gas chamber on January 22, 1963.

As the Quast case went forward, Jones began repeating claims that he had never confessed to killing Marguerita Bejarano, despite signing a three-page written confession. He told one reporter, "When you write your story, I want you to put two things in. First, I did not kill that little girl in Tucson and second, I've been kicked around by society ever since I was a kid and I don't care what happens to me now."[293]

A DEADLY LOVE TRIANGLE YIELDS TWO FUGITIVES

Fugitive(s): Glenn Everett Stewart and Edith Louise Schmidt
Wanted For: May 8, 1966, murder, Marion, Indiana
Captured: Stewart, May 24, 1966, Curtis, Arkansas
Schmidt, May 24, 1966, Marion, Indiana

Authorities in Marion, Indiana, didn't even know they had a murder to investigate until a young mother, twenty-five-year-old Edith L. Schmidt, approached police in Tennessee with an incredible story.

Schmidt, a resident of Marion, said she and her two children had been abducted days earlier and held against their will on a four-state trek from Indiana through Illinois, Missouri and Arkansas. Accompanied by her children, a seven-year-old boy and an eight-year-old girl, Mrs. Schmidt told the sheriff at White County, Tennessee, that a man had stabbed her husband to death, dismembered his body, and forced her and the children to flee with him.

Mrs. Schmidt said she had escaped her captor and fled to her parents' home near Gum Spring Mountain, Tennessee, but waited for several days before deciding to notify police of her husband's murder and her abduction. She said she paused out of intense fear that her attacker would find her hiding in Tennessee.

Police in Marion quickly confirmed most of the details of the story, finding what the Grant County coroner would describe as an "incredible scene," with the body of Larry Lee Schmidt, thirty, partially buried in the basement of his Marion home. "The arms and legs of the body were sawed off and found in an earthen basement of the victim's home," the *Indianapolis News* reported.[294]

Grant County coroner Dr. Russell W. Lavengood said Schmidt died of a massive stab wound to the heart. "His arms had been severed with a saw between the elbow and shoulder, and the legs had been cut off at the hips," Lavengood reported. He added that the arms had been placed inside rags and positioned next to the bottom of the torso, while the "legs had been tossed aside." Based on the level of decomposition, Lavengood estimated Larry Schmidt had been dead at least two weeks before his remains were found.[295]

A warrant for first-degree murder was immediately entered for Glenn Everett Stewart, a thirty-year-old Marion factory worker who lived near the Schmidts. Police in Arkansas were especially alerted, as Mrs. Schmidt detailed that she had escaped from Stewart near his hometown of Arkadelphia, Arkansas, on May 10 after he fell asleep.

Newspapers across the Midwest carried the photo of a distraught Mrs. Schmidt holding her face in her hands and detailing a "torturous trip" that covered two weeks, including hiding out in a wet Arkansas swamp. Mrs. Schmidt offered a frightening account of the ordeal she said she and her children had endured. She said her husband, employed at General Tire and Rubber Company in Marion, and Stewart, an employee at GM's Fisher Body Plant in Marion, had argued over an unpaid fifty-dollar debt.

"The killer forced Mrs. Schmidt to help dismember the body and clean up the blood," the woman told investigators. "After that, she told the sheriff that [Stewart] cut off a piece of flesh from her husband's body and put it on a plate and told her, 'It will happen to you too,' if she tried to escape."[296]

Based on Mrs. Schmidt's astonishing tale, police quickly surrounded the rural Arkadelphia, Arkansas home of Stewart's parents and successfully flushed him out of the home but didn't immediately apprehend him. As police searched for Stewart, Mrs. Schmidt was returned to Marion from Tennessee as a "material witness" in the case.

Once in Marion, Mrs. Schmidt elaborated on her story and claimed that Stewart barged into their home on April 30, demanding repayment of fifty dollars he alleged Larry Schmidt owed him. "[Stewart] scared me to death walking around the kitchen with that big knife in his hand," she said. "My husband came in and put down his lunch pail. The next thing I heard was a pounding in the bedroom."[297]

She recalled her husband calling out to her to call a doctor, and "I ran into the bedroom and saw my husband fall to the floor. He kept trying to get up, but [Stewart] kept kicking him back to the floor." Frightened into cooperation, Mrs. Schmidt said she kept her husband's death (and Stewart's hiding in her home) a secret, even when her brother visited the home the day after the murder. "That day, he wound up cutting his arms and legs off, and told me to look at [the body] real good because it would be me the next time."[298]

After the murder, Mrs. Schmidt said Stewart forced her and the children to accompany him to Arkansas. "We had no food," she said, describing how the children suffered. "We drank swamp water." Stewart was abusive to her children, Mrs. Schmidt said, forcing her continued compliance with his wishes. "He picked my little boy up and he'd shake him and beat him. I thought he would molest my daughter, but I broke that up, and I thought he would break my neck." Police noted, however, that the children appeared to be uninjured.[299]

Convinced that Stewart would find her in Tennessee after she and the children were able to slip away, "I waited until Sunday to talk to the sheriff because I was scared. I should have done something before now, but I couldn't take a chance of hurting those children."[300]

A day after Mrs. Schmidt retold her story to Indiana officials, Marion police announced that she had changed her story and now confessed that she had made it up and actually had assisted in killing her husband. She admitted that she had engaged in an extramarital affair with Stewart and had helped plan the murder before it was committed. She even corrected the date of the murder, confirming Larry Schmidt was killed on Mother's Day, May 8, rather than April 30, as she had originally said.

As Louise Schmidt was giving up the ghost in Marion, police in Arkansas were having success as well, finding Stewart hiding in a swampy area near Curtis, Arkansas (about ten miles south of his original hideout in Arkadelphia). Clark County sheriff R.W. Stevenson said Stewart was "completely exhausted, mosquito bitten and utterly defeated" when found.[301]

Once in custody, Stewart turned on Mrs. Schmidt the same way she had turned on him earlier. "I'll tell you fellows, I've lost faith in mankind too," he told Sheriff Stevenson. "I tried to help a friend and they turn around and stab me in the back."[302]

Louise Schmidt was tried and convicted on a charge of first-degree murder in Jay County in April 1967. She appealed her sentence, and in August 1973, the Indiana Supreme Court ruled 3-2 that her sentence should be amended to manslaughter, which carried a sentence of two to twenty-one years (rather than her original life sentence).[303]

A trial for Stewart was continually delayed as he underwent treatment at a state mental hospital, including receiving electric shock treatments. He was finally sentenced to two to twenty-one years in prison by a Grant County judge in December 1969. Stewart was convicted on a charge of being an accessory after the fact of murder, as the investigation determined Louise Schmidt had actually murdered her husband and asked Stewart to help dispose of the body.[304]

A DEADLY SHOOT-OUT STOPS THREE PRISON FUGITIVES

Fugitive(s): James H. Byrd, Arthur C. Murray and Howard Crooks

Wanted For: August 3, 1967, escape, Indiana State Prison, Michigan City, Indiana

August 10, 1967, murder of police officer, Lincoln, Nebraska

Captured: August 10, 1967, Lincoln, Nebraska

The day before three men scaled the walls of the Indiana State Prison at Michigan City, a special consultant arrived to assist prison officials in reassessing its security measures. It was help that arrived a little too late.

The prison warden blamed a shortage of guards for the escape, an especially embarrassing one: "The bold escape was made in daylight next to the administrative offices of the prison while officials inside were discussing security of the prison."[305]

At large were James H. Byrd, twenty-eight; Arthur C. Murray, thirty-three; and Howard Crooks, thirty-eight. Byrd was a lifer, convicted of a May 1963 robbery that severely injured a victim. Murray was serving a ten- to twenty-five-year sentence for robbery, while Crooks was in for a ten-year stint for commission of a crime with a deadly weapon.

The prisoners made their escape by crossing a twenty-foot metal extension ladder placed on the roof of a prison dormitory across to the forty-two-foot-high prison wall. They then climbed down a handmade rope at the wall and got away in a stolen car. "Prison officials said that the two towers from which they escaped could have been seen, but were not manned at the time of the escape," the *South Bend Tribune* reported. It reportedly took more than two hours for the warden to determine that three of the prison's 1,850 inmates were missing.

Interestingly, an hour before his escape, Crooks had attended a hearing to consider whether he should be granted trustee status to work in minimally secured areas of the prison grounds. His request was denied.

For Byrd, it was the fourth successful escape he had undertaken. In 1963, Byrd walked away from the Robert Long Hospital in Indianapolis after tying up two prison guards. Two years later, he also escaped from St. Anthony Hospital in Michigan City while receiving medical treatment. In September 1967, Byrd used a garden hose to climb the prison wall, but the hose broke, and Byrd fell and broke his leg—and was recaptured two weeks later in Nashville, Tennessee, sporting a cast on his leg.

A day after the men slipped away from the prison, police recovered the car they had stolen in Michigan City. It was parked on a city street in Salem, Indiana, 275 miles south of the prison, indicating that the men had made good progress.[306]

Nothing more was heard from the fugitives until August 10, 1967, when news crackled across the Associated Press wires in Indiana that the fugitive trio had engaged in a deadly gun battle with police at Lincoln, Nebraska, 570 miles west of the state prison. Killed in the gun fight was Lincoln police detective Paul Whitehead, thirty.

Byrd was wounded as police returned fire and was briefly hospitalized, while Murray and Crooks were captured without incident by other officers. The investigation showed Whitehead was shot while he and his partner, Detective Paul Merritt, investigated whether the men were driving a stolen car when they were stopped near Thirty-Seventh and O streets on Lincoln's near eastside. The check showed the car was reported stolen on August 5, 1967, from Pekin, Indiana.

Police said Whitehead was killed when shot at close range by a twelve-gauge shotgun. The father of three had been a detective less than a year when the late-night shooting occurred. "Authorities said the car was pulled over [and] Whitehead went to the driver's side of the vehicle and Merritt to the other. While checking the identification of one man, Byrd got out of the car and began firing….Whitehead and Merritt opened fire and the rear windshield [of the car] was hit by a shotgun blast and the trunk deck was peppered with revolver bullets," the *Lincoln Evening Journal* reported.[307]

The Hoosier fugitives weren't done. After the shootout, they sped off in the stolen car, with another Lincoln officer giving chase. The bandits finally stopped about ten blocks away, and two of the men fled on foot across a nearby field. Seventy-five police officers scoured the area for Murray and Crooks. Byrd, shot in the abdomen, had remained with the car. Murray and Crooks were eventually found hiding nearby about six hours after they fled.

The men were quickly linked to the armed robbery of a Carthage, Missouri liquor store two days before Lincoln officers engaged them in a gun battle. It was unclear where the men obtained the shotgun, although the liquor store robbery had resulted in a $500 take. Given the seriousness of the police officer's murder in Nebraska, Indiana authorities relented on any efforts to return the trio to Michigan City. Instead, criminal charges proceeded against the men in the Nebraska courts.

In January 1968, Byrd and Crooks both entered guilty pleas to a charge of second-degree murder. The charges were amended from first-degree murder in a plea agreement with Lancaster County district attorney Paul Douglas. Douglas said the murder charge against Murray would remain in place, as the investigation showed he was the one who fired the deadly shot at Detective Whitehead.[308]

A Lancaster County judge sentenced both men to the maximum penalty, life in prison.[309] Byrd's time in prison got off to a rocky start. Just months into his sentence, he was charged with attempted murder for stabbing another inmate in a violent prison fight.[310]

After months of wrangling back and forth, Murray decided to take the same path as his coconspirators and entered a plea of guilty to a charge of first-degree murder on November 4, 1968. Lancaster County judge Herbert A. Ronin wasted no time and promptly sentenced Murray to life in prison (sparing him the state's electric chair).

Murray's life sentence was a short one. On July 29, 1969, just eight months after being sentenced, Murray collapsed after taking a shower in a maximum-security area of the Nebraska Penitentiary. An autopsy showed the thirty-six-year-old man died of a heart attack, likely induced by prescribed tranquilizers he had recently started taking.[311]

In July 1971, Crooks and Byrd joined two other Nebraska prisoners in holding six prison guards hostage for two hours in an unsuccessful attempt to escape. They staged their effort during a retirement celebration for the prison's warden while guards were distracted. Both men had ten years added to their existing life sentences.[312]

On July 14, 1983, Crooks was apparently not done trying to get free. Despite his escape attempt in 1971, Nebraska prison officials had granted him trustee status, which he exploited fully. Crooks walked away undetected from a trustee assignment in a construction area of the state penitentiary. He was eventually apprehended near Mitchell, Indiana, on August 10, 1983.[313]

During his nearly one month of freedom, Crooks had abducted a sixteen-year-old girl from a grocery store parking lot in Council Bluffs, Iowa, and was found holding her when apprehended in Indiana. The girl was later hospitalized for physical and emotional injuries and was allegedly raped by the now fifty-four-year-old Crooks.[314]

Crooks was convicted of abduction and rape in March 1984 and given a new life sentence, this time in the Iowa Penitentiary. His victim and her family later sued the State of Nebraska for its inability to keep Crooks behind bars.[315] Iowa officials had the same problems Indiana and Nebraska had experienced with Crooks, as he used a handmade key to unlock his leg shackles while using the restroom in a hospital at Fort Madison, Iowa, in April 1985. He was stopped by a prison guard, however, before getting free.[316]

THE PHYSICALLY FIT FUGITIVE

Fugitive(s): George Edward Blue
Wanted For: July 11, 1968, bank robbery, Evansville, Indiana
November 26, 1968, bank robbery, Atwood, Indiana
Captured: March 28, 1969, Chicago, Illinois

Perhaps reflecting the era in which it was published, the FBI's Most Wanted poster for Indiana fugitive George Edward Blue made special mention of some particular personal features about the man.

He was wanted for the July 11, 1968 armed robbery of the Old National Bank in Evansville, Indiana, and the bulletin from the FBI interestingly emphasized that Blue was a muscular Black man who engaged in bodybuilding, ate healthy foods and enjoyed the company of White women.

"Blue, a Negro, regularly lifts weights and is a muscular man," United Press International reported. "He is known to eat health foods and vitamin preparations as well. The wanted man is described as polite, soft-spoken and grammatical in his speech. He frequents racially integrated night clubs."[317]

The FBI warning issued on February 25, 1969, included the standard warning that Blue, thirty-nine, had been armed in the past and should be considered "armed and dangerous."[318] He was a native of Boonville, Indiana, and the FBI believed Blue was still in the Indiana area.[319]

The bank robbery near the University of Evansville campus committed by Blue and a White suspect netted the pair $5,670. News reporters seemed to have some fun with stories about the case, noting that the robbers were White and Black and escaped in a stolen white-and-black car.[320]

Four days after the robbery, Evansville authorities picked up two city women, Lillian Berry, thirty-six, and Karen Fay Husk, twenty-one, both identified as White women. Police charged them with being "accessories after the fact" for allegedly driving the getaway car.

As more time passed, police became concerned that Blue would become more and more desperate to avoid returning to jail. He previously served twelve years in prison in Indiana on other robbery charges. In fact, the July 1968 Evansville robbery occurred less than a month after Blue completed his probation on previous charges.[321]

Blue was known to rely heavily on his female friends for both shelter and support while he was a fugitive. True to form, Chicago police apprehended Blue on March 29, 1969, in the company of a new girlfriend, twenty-four-year-old Mary Ann Davis. Police held Davis as a material witness for another bank robbery attributed to Blue and retrieved a .38-caliber pistol from her purse.[322]

Police found Blue as he was waiting to board a bus at the Greyhound bus station in downtown Chicago. When placed under arrest, Blue was armed with a loaded revolver but offered no resistance. It wasn't until Blue was under arrest that police named him as one of their prime suspects in a spectacular November 26, 1968 bank robbery in the tiny Kosciusko County community of Atwood, Indiana. At the time, the story of theft from the Etna Bank branch at Atwood gained notice statewide: "Two gun-wielding men entered a bank branch manager's house Tuesday night and then forced him to drive to the bank and open a vault, while his son was held hostage. They escaped with just over $4,000."[323]

The *South Bend Tribune* reported the "masked robbers" forced their way into the rural home of Larry Hoffer and tied up and gagged three members of the Hoffer family. From there, they forced Hoffer to drive to his bank branch and effect the theft. "Hoffer was forced to drive back to his house after the robbery where he and his son were also tied and gagged," noted the *South Bend Tribune* account. Hoffer told police one of the men was a Black man who held a snub-nosed revolver in his face and ordered him, "Get in the house, do as you are told and nobody will get hurt."[324]

"The robbery appeared to be well-planned as the two men had brought their own rope and gagged their victims with tape," the *Tribune* reported. Bound and gagged but otherwise unhurt were Hoffer's wife, Marilyn, their two daughters, ages five and three, and an eight-year-old son. "Mrs. Hoffer said her children remained very calm, even the smaller ones, as she told them to 'sit down and everything will be alright.'"[325]

Hoffer said the men also searched his home extensively and said he tried to bluff the men into thinking the bank's safe could not be opened because of a time-device lock. The men were not deterred and told Hoffer, "Don't do anything or we'll shoot your kid."[326]

On December 11, 1969, U.S. District Court judge Robert A. Grant sentenced Blue to twenty years in a federal penitentiary for the Atwood bank robbery. He received an additional fifteen-year sentence for the Evansville robbery. During his sentencing, Blue told the judge that after he was incarcerated as a young man in 1948: "I never got my feet on the ground since. You might call me a hustler."[327]

6

1970-79

A FUGITIVE BECOMES A COP WHILE ON THE RUN

Fugitive(s): Norman K. Bevins
Wanted For: August 1969, child sexual assault, Greenfield, Indiana
March 1970, bail jumping, Greenfield, Indiana
Captured: May 5, 1983, Jenkins, Kentucky

Whenever a fugitive is apprehended, the first question almost always is what was the fugitive doing during his time on the run?

In the case of forty-four-year-old Norman K. Bevins, who became a fugitive in March 1970 for failure to appear for a trial on charges of statutory rape, he spent a portion of his time on the run as a Kentucky police officer. Originally charged in August 1969 in a case involving a twelve-year-old New Palestine girl, Bevins skipped town just as his trial was to get underway at the Hancock County Courthouse in Greenfield.[328]

Bevins had always denied the charges against him and fired his attorney in the case just days before the trial was to start.[329]

Beyond the curiosity of whatever became of Bevins is the question of how serious was the manhunt for him to begin with? Initially, Hancock County authorities suggested that Bevins had fled to West Virginia, where he might have family and friends residing. They had that part of the story wrong.

It wasn't as if Bevins seemed to be trying that hard to hide. For two years, Bevins worked as a patrol officer for the police department in tiny Fleming-Neon, Kentucky. Located 330 miles south of Greenfield and nestled in Letcher County near the Kentucky-Virginia border, Fleming-Neon has never had more than eight hundred citizens. The Elkhorn Coal Company established the town for its workers and it was named for George W. Fleming, the coal company's first president.

During his tenure on the police department, Bevins even made news following a December 20, 1979 shooting in which he was injured. As the Associated Press reported at the time, "A policeman was wounded before dawn today when he surprised burglars attempting to break into a drug store in Neon. State police said policeman Norman Bevins, was hit in the upper left arm by shotgun pellets."[330]

The burglary, at the town's Walgreens pharmacy, was discovered by Bevins while he was on routine patrol at about 5:15 a.m. "[Bevins] observed that the intruders were armed with a shotgun and a small caliber weapon," the AP reported. Despite being struck by shotgun pellets, Bevins was not hospitalized.[331]

Also during his time in Kentucky, Bevins managed a local Moose lodge and gained a new indictment in June 1981 for two counts of unlawfully transporting firearms and unlawfully selling guns without a firearms license. It was the new firearms warrant—and not the 1970 bail jumping warrant—that prompted Kentucky authorities to act. "Kentucky authorities, aware of the outstanding Indiana fugitive warrant, located Bevins recently in a trailer court outside of Jenkins, Kentucky," the *Indianapolis News* reported.[332]

Hancock County sheriff Nick Gulling said Bevins had avoided arrest for so long because he had not been "hounded" enough. "It was just one of those things that never got done for a couple of years," Gulling said.[333]

Back in Fleming-Neon, the city's police chief, Astor Gibson, confirmed Bevins had been on the three-man force in 1978–79 and was hired by a former mayor. "Neon is a small town, and when the mayor leaves office, the police department goes with him," Astor said. Bevins and his wife were respected in the community, and from all indications, he had been a good police officer.[334]

His time on the run, however, had not been easy. As *Indianapolis Star* reporters Joseph Konz and William Sedivy noted, "During his flight from the law, Bevins and his family lived like nomads along the Kentucky-Virginia border. Sheriff Gulling, who drove Bevins back to Greenfield, described him as "real friendly" and said he believed "he just wanted to get it over with. I got the impression he'd been living with this thing hanging over his head a long time and felt it was time to get it straightened out once and for all."[335]

Despite the long gap between the original alleged rape, 1969, and his apprehension, 1983, prosecutors said they still had a good case against Bevins. That turned out to be a lofty assessment, as jurors acquitted Bevins on the statutory rape charge following a one-day trial on September 25, 1984. Now age forty-six and battling cancer, Bevins told reporter Konz, "I'm elated at the whole thing. This has been a terrible ordeal for my family, but they've stuck by me through it all. I guess I have a little more faith in justice."[336]

THIRTY-FIVE YEARS OF FUGITIVE FREEDOM

Fugitive(s): Linda Darby
Wanted For: March 13, 1972, escape, Indiana Women's Prison, Indianapolis, Indiana
Captured: October 12, 2007, Pulaski, Tennessee

On a spring evening, just before dark on March 13, 1972, Linda Darby participated in a volleyball game among inmates of the Indiana Women's Prison. When the game came to a close at about 8:30 p.m., all of the women returned to their cells—all except Darby.

Soon, prison officials confirmed that Darby had unexpectedly scaled a barbed-wire fence surrounding the prison in a residential neighborhood east of downtown Indianapolis. Prison superintendent Grace Kwolek expressed surprise about Darby's escape because she had been "a good prisoner" who was intelligent. "She would get depressed sometimes, like the rest of the prisoners, but she never gave us any indication of anything like this," Kwolek said.[337]

At the time she went missing, Darby was twenty-eight years old and in the second year of her life sentence for the shotgun slaying of her Lake County husband. Under Indiana law at the time, she would have to serve at least fifteen years before any reconsideration of her life sentence could be undertaken.

That spring day was the last anyone heard of Darby—and it seemed she would remain a fugitive forever. That was until 2007, when the Indiana General Assembly approved changes in state statutes and funding for a special fugitives unit to be formed to allow the Department of Correction to track down its escaped inmates. Darby was near the top of that list.

On October 12, 2007—a full thirty-five years since Darby escaped the Indianapolis prison—a combined task force of federal, Indiana and Tennessee authorities surrounded Darby's simple home near downtown Pulaski, Tennessee. Knocking on the door, they met a now sixty-four-year-old woman using the name Linda Joy McElroy. Linda McElroy, however, was in fact Linda Darby.

"Authorities said Darby had raised a family and apparently led a quiet, crime-free life in Tennessee," the Associated Press reported. Under arrest, Darby told reporters that she was innocent of the 1970 murder of her husband that had gained her the life sentence to begin with.[338]

Linda told investigators that when she got away from the prison, her first thought was to try to return to her children, but she worried that would mean she would be recaptured immediately. Instead, she knocked on the door of a random Eastside Indianapolis home and asked for help, explaining her cuts from the barbed wire as evidence of domestic abuse. While staying with the Indianapolis family, she met Joe McElroy, who would eventually become her third husband.

Though more than three decades had passed, old-timers in Lake County and all of northwest Indiana remembered the gruesome details of the murder of twenty-five-year-old Charles R. Darby, which occurred on March 3, 1970. Charles Darby was Linda's second husband and was found wrapped in garment bags on his bed after firefighters put out a fire at his simple five-room track home located at 7545 Beech Avenue in Hammond.

An autopsy showed that Charles had been shot once in the side with a shotgun—likely while he slept—and was then partially wrapped in a garment bag. Gasoline was spread over his body and around the house and then lit. Firefighters were immediately notified of the 12:30 a.m. fire because of an explosion that accompanied the flames, knocking the small house slightly off its foundation.[339]

Linda Darby and her five children were not at home at the time of the fire, police said, and neighbors indicated that Darby told neighbors they were going to visit relatives in Ashby, Kentucky. Interestingly, the day before the murder and fire, Charles Darby had placed a classified advertisement in local newspapers disclaiming any new debts incurred by his wife, "usually a first step in divorce or separation proceedings," the *Hammond Times* reported.[340]

The fire in which Charles died was actually the second one at the home in a year. In April 1969, another fire gutted the interior of the home, with a cause never determined by local fire investigators. The "bad luck" and "odd occurrences" in the Darby family also included a fake obituary placed in the *Hammond Times* claiming that Linda and Charles Darby had been fatally injured in a car accident at Nashville. The report was later determined to be fake, and Linda Darby told police the family had been receiving death threats.

The *Hammond Times* ran a photo of the burned-out bed in which Charles had died, dragged into the front yard of the home during the firefight. It also noted, "Linda Darby, described as a meticulous housekeeper and good mother, would occasionally use a neighbor's phone and had told the neighbor she was going to Kentucky without her husband."[341]

A day after the murder was discovered, Linda Darby talked freely with police investigators and reporters about her life. She said recent events had scared both of them: "There's nothing that Charles or I have done to bring on all of this." Vandalism to their car and a backyard fence set afire were originally attributed to delinquent youths. "At first we had thought maybe it was a teenager playing some kind of prank," Linda said. That changed, however, after the fake obituary for the couple appeared in the newspaper.[342]

Charles Darby, a self-employed subcontractor, specialized in installing aluminum siding on homes in northwest Indiana and suburban Chicago communities. Linda Darby wondered whether her husband was angering local unions who competed with him for construction jobs. "They wouldn't do this sort of thing just because the men don't belong [to a union] would they?" she asked.[343]

Despite the local advertisement about the couple's debts, Linda Darby denied the couple were planning to be divorced or separated and said they had just placed a down payment on a home in Chesterton, Indiana. She said her husband wanted to move to a more rural area because "he just loved woods and farms" and often attended what she called "high stakes" poker games at a Hammond hotel.

Linda Darby explained that she was driving back to Hammond at the time of the murder and fire. She said she had made it as far as Valparaiso, just thirty minutes from her home at Hammond. She told police she stopped at a motel in Valparaiso for the night with her children because she was tired (even though she had already driven almost three hundred miles from Kentucky). It was a curious story.

Adding to her odd behavior, Linda quickly left Hammond to return to Kentucky, presumably to attend her murdered husband's funeral in his hometown. In the meantime, Lake County authorities succeeded in obtaining a warrant for Linda's arrest on a charge of murder and followed her to Kentucky to affect her arrest. The charge against Linda indicated a witness identified her as the woman who purchased two gallons of gasoline on the night of the fire, in addition to a shotgun hidden behind a vending machine in the motel where Linda and her children had stayed that night.[344]

Despite the warrant for her arrest, Linda was allowed to attend her husband's funeral and was even granted a temporary bond from a Kentucky jail. Linda's father, Chester Adams of Catlettsburg, Kentucky, said his daughter was innocent. Adams said he had visited his daughter in jail and reported, "She's a very upset little girl, very unhappy" and that "she insisted that she didn't kill her husband."[345]

It would take two more months, but Hammond authorities finally succeeded in getting Linda Darby returned to Lake County, where she was housed at the county jail. In June 1970, Lake County Jail warden Harry Selin reported that Linda was confirmed to be two months pregnant, having become pregnant in the weeks since her husband was found dead in March.[346]

The trial for Linda Darby got underway in September 1970 but included no witnesses called by the defense. Prosecutors, meanwhile, produced a variety of damning witnesses, including tearful testimony from Linda's nine-year-old daughter from a previous marriage, Terri Lynn Dixon. The young girl testified that she heard her mother leave their motel room on the night of the murder after she thought everyone was asleep. She returned between 12:30 and 1:00 a.m., she said, just as the fire was being reported. She further testified that her mother had made a strong point of telling a neighbor they were leaving town for a few days and allowed her to hurriedly get her favorite watch out of their home before heading for Kentucky.

Terri Dixon testified that her mother had threatened her into silence. "She told me if I told anybody [about her leaving the motel], she wouldn't buy me anything else new."[347]

Jurors deliberated just seventy-five minutes before convicting Linda, and she was sentenced to life in prison. She was sent to the Indiana Women's Prison in Indianapolis to serve her time.[348]

In 2007, as her long fugitive run came to an end, those who knew her in Pulaski, Tennessee, were stunned to learn of her past. Giles County sheriff Kyle Helton said he knew Linda and her husband, Joe McElroy, who once operated an antique shop in the community.

"As far as I know, she never had any criminal history after she came here," Sheriff Helton said. "She never got into any trouble. She led a flawless life."

Linda's neighbors and acquaintances were equally supportive of her. Her seventy-seven-year-old neighbor, Alex Harwell, said, "She was real nice. It just makes you wonder: When someone's been out of trouble for 35 years, what's the point of putting them in jail?"[349]

Another person who knew Linda for more than twenty years, Bill Hatfield, said, "She wouldn't hurt a flea. She's cleaned our house for 15 years and has a key to the house. I'd let her in tomorrow. She's never done anything but help people. She used to care for my elderly parents, staying at night, and she had the full run of the house. She cared for my mother like she was her own mother."[350]

As expected, Charles Darby's family had a different view of the situation. Their loved one, a Vietnam War veteran, was just twenty-five years old when he was killed. His sister, Alice Robinette, told a reporter that his death had devastated her parents, and all felt relief that Linda was under arrest.

"We are Christians. We don't believe in revenge," Robinette said. "But I was glad they caught her. I just hope they don't let her go again. She needs to pay for her crime. She got to live. [My brother] didn't."[351]

Darby lost an April 2012 appeal of her sentence and, as of this writing, still must serve a minimum of fifteen years before she can be considered for any parole.

A DECADE OF CLEAN LIVING IS FINALLY ENOUGH

Fugitive(s): Mae Dell Smith
Wanted For: April 9, 1972, escape, Indiana Women's Prison, Indianapolis, Indiana
Captured: May 13, 1982, Colorado Springs, Colorado

When questioned by FBI agents as a witness in a robbery investigation, "Greta Daniels" was keeping a secret that would soon be discovered.

Agents interrogating her soon learned through fingerprints that her real name was Mae Dell Smith, and she had been a fugitive from the Indiana Woman's Prison in Indianapolis for a decade.

In Colorado Springs, Colorado, where Smith was held on pending extradition orders in Indiana, her public defender, Jim Sawyer, said she had lived "a damned exemplary life" for ten years in Colorado and deserved a break. Smith was also counting on her good record to earn her some credit. Speaking from a cell in the El Paso County Jail, Smith said FBI agents had "reneged on a pledge to help her fight extradition in exchange for information on the robbery."

"I guess I didn't tell them what they wanted to know, so that's why they haven't helped me," Smith said.

The FBI refused to comment on Smith's claims of help from its agents. The FBI did confirm it had questioned Smith about any knowledge she might have of a robbery and said she voluntarily disclosed her real identity after being fingerprinted because "I knew they would eventually learn my identity."[352]

Smith added, "The FBI said they would call Indiana and get it fixed up, but as you see, they didn't. I'm just sitting here waiting for them to come and get me from Indiana."[353]

Now thirty-two years old, Smith was just twenty-one when she and four other inmates overpowered a sixty-year-old female jail matron at the historic prison in the Woodruff Place neighborhood of Indianapolis. The jailbreak hadn't generated big headlines in Indianapolis at the time. Eventually, four of the five women (except Smith) were apprehended in the area and returned to prison.

The other four escapees were identified as Geneva Anderson, twenty-six; Penny Fishers, nineteen; Pat E. Holt, twenty-six; and Mary H. Wells, twenty-nine.

Smith, serving a two- to ten-year sentence for violating the 1935 Narcotics Act, and the others, were believed to have climbed over a back fence at the prison bordering nearby East Michigan Street, the *Indianapolis Star* reported.[354]

Smith's court-appointed attorney in Colorado, Sawyer, said he had sent letters to both Indiana governor Robert D. Orr and Colorado governor Richard Lamm, asking them to intervene and reject efforts to return her to Indiana. While in Colorado, "she has been a good citizen," Sawyer said. "The big reason I'm upset and perhaps other people are upset is the fact that the woman walked away from the very tail end of a sentence on a narcotics charge 10 years ago, and has led a damned exemplary life since then."[355]

Smith told investigators she had lived in both Denver and Colorado Springs in the years since she fled Indiana. She claimed that she had found work in a variety of fields, including as a nurse's aide, draftsman, map maker, geological technician and a model. She had also taken broadcast journalism classes at Pikes Peak Community College for two years.

Asked about how she had stayed out of trouble for a decade after escaping, she told a reporter, "I had learned if you do crime, you end up in prison, and I didn't want to go back there."[356]

As she awaited extradition, Smith was married while still incarcerated. She continued to express hope that she would win release so she could complete her associate's degree. In November 1982, Smith got her wish, as Governor Orr announced that Indiana would not extradite Smith to Hoosier soil. "As long as Mae Dell Smith continues to live without running afoul of the law, she probably has nothing to worry about," said Clem Engle, Indiana assistant attorney general.[357]

Smith, whose new married name was Rivera, told a reporter, "I'm just happy it's over. I don't want to feel bitter or anything toward anybody. I've learned a lot from the experience, basically, not to get involved on the wrong side of the law. I feel as if I've had an experience that very few people have."[358]

AMERICA'S "FIRST" MOST WANTED

Fugitive(s): David James Roberts
Wanted For: January 20, 1974, murder, New Whiteland, Indiana
November 15, 1974, murder, rape and kidnapping, Indianapolis, Indiana
October 24, 1986, escape from prison custody, San Pierre, Indiana
Captured: February 11, 1988, Staten Island, New York

In October 1986, Rupert Murdoch launched FOX, a fourth television network in the United States, designed to compete with the established players, ABC, CBS and NBC. That same month, David James Roberts became a fugitive from justice in Indiana.

The advent of the FOX television network was obviously bigger news. Strung together by a handful of leftover VHS stations and Murdoch-owned affiliates across the nation, FOX was attempting to do what few had succeeded at—compete with the nation's oldest networks. NBC television first went on the air in 1939, CBS followed in 1941 and ABC in 1948. The last fourth network to try its luck—DuMont—survived only from 1942 until 1956.

Murdoch and FOX were determined and offered a variety of edgy TV shows meant to draw a younger, more urban audience. Among the first shows offered on the network was *America's Most Wanted*, originally aired as a thirty-minute program, premiering on Sunday, February 7, 1988. It was hosted by crime victim turned crime fighter John Walsh, and the first case profiled on the show was that of David James Roberts.

Roberts, who was living in New York City under the name Robert Lord, happened to be hospitalized that evening and was apparently watching TV. He offered little resistance when police finally reached him on February 11, 1988, and placed him under arrest as an Indiana fugitive from multiple murder, rape, kidnapping and arson charges. He had successfully eluded justice since October 24, 1986.

It was on an autumn afternoon just before 3:00 p.m., when Roberts regained his freedom. As armed guards were returning him to the Indiana State Prison at Michigan City after he received medical treatment at Wishard Memorial Hospital in Indianapolis, he escaped. The prison vehicle carrying Roberts was within fifty miles of the prison when the guards decided to stop for food, using a drive-through window at a McDonald's restaurant along U.S. 421 near San Pierre (Starke County), southeast of Valparaiso.

"The guards had stopped for lunch and loosened Roberts' chains so he could eat," the *Chicago Tribune* reported. "Roberts then pulled a hidden pistol, seized a handgun from one of the guards, handcuffed the two and ordered them to get in the back seat of the vehicle." Prison spokesman Herbert Newkirk explained, "It appears he was able to obtain a handgun somewhere on the trip. He took the officers' transport vehicle, their uniform shirts, caps and firearms."[359]

Roberts drove the guards to Hammond, where they were able to escape after Roberts left the vehicle unattended for a few moments. The state prison vehicle was later found abandoned at a South Shore train station in East Chicago, where it was believed Roberts boarded a Chicago-bound train.

The officers later told their bosses that Roberts had been strip-searched before leaving the prison to go to the hospital but was not searched again after leaving the hospital. He was briefly left alone in a men's room at Wishard, they said, and investigators believe this is where he retrieved a gun, placed there for him by an unknown accomplice.

In Indianapolis, state correctional officials were red-faced. Roberts was a feared character in central Indiana, where he had been convicted of crimes that had left four people dead. "This guy's a very good talker, very neat appearing and I consider him dangerous, very manipulative," said Vaughn Overstreet, a spokesman for the Indiana Department of Correction. "He's had 13 years to think about [this escape], and it was pretty well planned."[360]

Roberts had always been a well-planned, coordinated criminal. His original crime, the murder of William E. Patrick, twenty-five; his wife, Ann, twenty-three; and their one-year-old daughter, Heidi, was carried out with deadly precision. All three of the Patricks were found dead in January 1974, after firefighters put out an early morning arson fire at their home at 851 Princeton Drive in New Whiteland (Johnson County).

"Investigators found the bodies of Patrick and his wife on the floor of the family room after the blaze had been extinguished," the *Franklin Daily Journal* reported. "Firemen rescued the child from her crib in a rear bedroom after breaking out a window, but she was dead on arrival at Johnson County Memorial Hospital. The child reportedly died of smoke inhalation." A strong odor of gasoline was noted at the home, and investigators said they found a five-gallon gasoline can on the floor near Patrick's body. "The woman's body was lying next to her husband's on the floor," the *Daily Journal* noted.[361]

An autopsy was conducted on the Patricks, but the results were not fully disclosed. Dr. Harley Palmer, the Johnson County coroner, said the two adults were dead before the fire was set, though. The fire was confirmed to be arson. "The deaths are just unexplainable at this time," said Johnson County prosecutor Joe Van Valer.[362]

Just over a week after the deadly fire, Johnson County authorities announced they had arrested Roberts, then thirty years old and listing an Indianapolis address, and were charging him only with the arson death of little Heidi Patrick. Since an exact cause of death was still not determined for her parents, no initial charges were entered for him on that. (He eventually would be charged with all three deaths, as well as arson.)

Identified as a parolee from the Pendleton Reformatory, "Roberts had been under surveillance since January 23 when detectives learned of a possible motive which would have linked Roberts to the mysterious arson fire." Van Valer confirmed that "investigators had learned [William] Patrick was employed at the downtown Indianapolis Sears automotive store, and was a witness in a pending theft trial in Marion County against Roberts. It was alleged that Roberts was seen by Patrick as having taken four tires and an automotive exhaust system from the auto store in October 1973." Patrick had installed the new items on Roberts's car earlier in the day and parked it in the lot waiting for pickup. Roberts came, however, and drove the car off without paying for the parts and labor.[363]

Witness statements provided to police placed Roberts's 1970 Buick Rivera in the neighborhood of the Parker home on the night of the fire, and another witness identified Roberts as having asked for directions to Princeton Drive in New Whiteland. Van Valer told a reporter, "It was a very sophisticated homicide, but a very poor arson job."[364]

Roberts was indicted for the murders of the Parker family in March 1974 but was surprisingly released on bond by a Johnson County judge. While out on bond, he abducted and raped a nineteen-year-old Indianapolis woman on November 15, 1974, and left her infant child to die of exposure along a city street. He was expected to be tried on those charges once the Parker murder trial was completed.

Also while out on bond for the spectacular charges pending against him in adjacent Johnson County, Roberts somehow gained employment in a job training program operated by the City of Indianapolis. It was while he was on the city payroll that Roberts was accused of abducting the young woman and her baby on the Westside of Indianapolis.

Detectives said Robert's latest victim was driving her car westbound on Thirty-Fourth Street when she stopped for a red light at High School Road. "[Roberts] then forced his way into her car. Her baby, whom she had just picked up from a babysitter's home, was on the front seat of the car. She said the man took her to a nearby church parking lot where he raped her," the *Indianapolis News* reported.[365]

The woman said her attacker drove her car to the city's Eastside but not before he raped her again and stole two dollars from her purse. "Her assailant then forced her to get into the trunk of her car, and the man drove for a few minutes before stopping," the *News* account relayed. "The car was abandoned…and the woman began screaming for help by beating on the trunk lid with a tire iron. She was heard by a nearby resident who called police."[366]

When officers located her, the woman's baby was missing from the car. Police engaged an exhaustive search of the city, until an emergency call was received at 8:00 a.m. Friday morning from a boy indicating he had found a baby's body lying along the 4500 block of East Thirty-Eighth Street. "Police believe the baby was put out of the car when the woman said her assailant was gone for about five minutes, which was about 4 a.m.," the *News* noted.[367]

Marion County coroner Dennis Nicholas ruled that the six-month-old child died of exposure to cold temperatures after being in the elements for hours. There were no cuts or bruises on the child's body, clad only in a nightgown. "A light blue blanket, which the mother had previously wrapped around her son, was found next to the body," Nicholas said.[368]

Johnson County sheriff Jack Means (concerned that a judge had let Roberts out on bond) saw a description of the rape suspect on Indianapolis

TV stations and called Marion County authorities and suggested they check on Roberts. A photograph of Roberts was shown to the rape victim, and she positively identified him as her assailant. He was arrested without incident.

Roberts's trial for the New Whiteland murders finally got underway in November 1975, with the case moved to Steuben County, almost two hundred miles away from Johnson County and the Indianapolis area, where it had received significant publicity. The November trial was the second one for Roberts—a trial started in July 1975 ended quickly when a mistrial was declared before jury selection was completed.

Following a six-day trial in Angola, Indiana, on November 17, 1975, Roberts was found guilty of six counts of murder, arson and burglary related to the death of the Parker family. He was immediately returned to Indianapolis so that another trial could commence—this one for the abduction and rape of a city woman and the death of her infant son. Just after Thanksgiving, however, a second mistrial on the matter was declared after three jurors became ill (one of whom engaged in a disruptive courtroom outburst).[369]

As plans got underway for a third trial in the Marion County abduction, rape and murder case, a Steuben County judge sentenced Roberts to die in the state's electric chair for his murder of the Parker family. His sentence was later converted to life in prison.[370] Finally, on January 13, 1977, a Marion County jury found Roberts guilty of two counts of kidnapping, one count of murder and one count of rape. "Roberts displayed emotion by pounding his fists on the table and shaking his head when the verdict was read, and then broke into tears," the *Indianapolis News* reported. He received a second life sentence for his newest convictions.[371]

Despite the best efforts of law enforcement and the courts to convict and confine Roberts, he had slipped away. From October 1986 to February 1988, Indiana authorities did not know exactly where Roberts was. Unknown to them, he had hitchhiked from Chicago and landed in New York City. Showing up at one of the city's homeless shelters, he quickly impressed workers there with his potential and mannerly way of speaking and acting.

The *New York Daily News*, along with all national media, reported heavily on the capture of Roberts as a result of the *America's Most Wanted* TV report. Staten Island Episcopal bishop Patrick Ahern said [Roberts] was "a gentleman and a superb supervisor. To the homeless men he helped, [Roberts] was a godsend."[372]

Known to his colleagues on Staten Island as Robert Lord, the respect held for him did not prevent as many as seventy-five people in the New York City area from calling the *America's Most Wanted* hotline, certain that the man they knew as Robert Lord was actually the wanted fugitive killer David James Roberts.

Roberts first came to the homeless shelter in November 1986, worked as a volunteer and was eventually hired in April 1987 as a supervisor. He was so trusted that just a week before he was apprehended, the shelter had sent him to speak to a class of sixth grade students about how they could help the homeless.

A "PORN KING" BECOMES AN INDIANA FUGITIVE

Fugitive(s): Michael Thevis
Wanted For: April 28, 1978, escape, Floyd County Jail, New Albany, Indiana
October 25, 1978, double murder, Atlanta, Georgia
Captured: November 9, 1978, Bloomfield, Connecticut

Michael Thevis was an unusually charismatic fellow for a guy who made his living producing and distributing pornography. He was dubbed the "Sultan of Smut," according to *Newsweek* magazine.

The FBI believed it was his friendly personality and generosity with his personal fortune—estimated to be in the hundreds of millions of dollars—that aided Thevis from walking away unmolested from the Floyd County Jail in New Albany in April 1978.

Held in New Albany temporarily at the conclusion of a civil lawsuit against him in nearby Louisville, Kentucky, Thevis was scheduled to be returned to a federal prison hospital in Springfield, Missouri. It was a transfer that would never occur, as he disappeared until apprehended seven months later wearing a costume and trying to withdraw a lot of money from a Connecticut bank.

Federal authorities and police in Georgia believe that in the months he was free as a fugitive from the county jail in Indiana, Thevis took care of a key witness against him in pending federal obscenity and RICO (Racketeer Influences and Corrupt Organizations) trials that would put him away for life.

The witness, Roger Dean Undill, was Thevis's former trusted partner and developer of highly profitable twenty-five-cent vending machines that played porno films in thousands of adult bookstores across the nation. Underhill, fifty, was fatally wounded by shotgun blasts during an ambush on him and another man in suburban Atlanta on October 25, 1978. Also killed was an investor who had the bad luck of being in Underhill's company that day, identified as grocery store owner Ike N. Galanti, forty-eight, of Atlanta.

Underhill was "the man authorities had been counting on to be a key witness in the murder and racketeering trials of escaped pornographer Michael Thevis," the *Atlanta Constitution* reported. "Underhill's death greatly weakens two criminal cases pending against Thevis, authorities confirmed."[373]

Thevis, already a suspect in the shooting death of a rival porn operator, Kenneth "Jap" Hanna, who was killed in 1970 (his body dumped in the trunk of a car at the Atlanta airport), remained at large. Underhill, investigators said, was preparing to videotape more than three hundred pages of deposition testimony to be used in prosecuting Thevis.

Federal investigators estimated that Thevis controlled more than 40 percent of the "peep shows" and adult bookstores across the nation, valued at hundreds of millions of dollars. He had formed more than two hundred corporations, the feds said, some regular mail-order companies selling fruit and cheese baskets and others distributing mail-order pornography out of Atlanta. Thevis, unlike other underworld characters, did not shy away from media attention, including telling how he went from a poor newsstand operator to a major porn figure.

"I sensed [in the 1960s] that something was happening with reader demands," Thevis told one reporter. "Books that dealt with sex didn't stay on the shelves very long. So don't come at me with the business that I created the demand for sex books or sex magazines. The public, certain portions of it at least, created the demand."[374]

Back in New Albany, angry FBI officials were demanding an investigation into how Thevis could have gotten away so easily, and why he was gone for several hours before the FBI was notified. Thevis had just lost the civil case in Louisville, following a seven-day trial, with the jury ordering him to pay $687,000 for the arson fire that destroyed a rival's warehouse.

Although Thevis was reportedly wearing a leg brace and walking with a cane during the entire time he was in Indiana, FBI officials were probing whether he had paid off doctors for a diagnosis that would allow him to be housed at a prison hospital. "I assume it was a planned escape with confederates available," said U.S. attorney James Baker in Atlanta, who was heading the federal case against Thevis. Baker said FBI agents had arrested Thevis's girlfriend, Patricia McClean, who had visited him in the Floyd County Jail on three consecutive days before he escaped.[375]

Baker complained that the Floyd County sheriff waited too long to notify federal authorities that Thevis was gone. Baker questioned whether Floyd County sheriff Alex Watkins was too distracted by the sheriff's election going on in the county—one in which he was backing his brother (Kenneth Watkins) for the office he was term limited from keeping. Baker even called out local authorities for the fact that it was more than an hour before jailers knew Thevis was gone (about 9:00 p.m.) and the FBI wasn't called until 3:30 a.m. the following morning.

"It is my understanding there is an election coming up," Baker said. "It was reported to me [by FBI agents in Louisville] that one of the reasons for the impending delay in notifying us was the election and the embarrassment the escape might cause the sheriff and his brother." Sheriff Watkins angrily dismissed that claim, telling a reporter, "The election has not a damned thing to do with it." Baker also questioned why Sheriff Watkins had notified Thevis's personal attorney hours before notifying the FBI. "I find it strange," Baker said, indicating he would push for an investigation.[376]

The investigation would later show that Thevis had enjoyed a rather comfortable arrangement in the Floyd County Jail, which held only fifty prisoners. The one-story structure was guarded at times by only one guard, who was stationed at the Sheriff's Department front desk in the county building. Supervision, it seemed, was lacking.

Reporters also speculated that Thevis had handsomely rewarded some of the locals to allow him to use a chief sheriff deputy's office to make personal phone calls for as long as three and four hours at a time. Thevis was using one of those phones—in an office along an unsecured hallway of the jail—when he slipped away.

Sheriff Watkins defended his procedures but admitted he had removed a pay phone for inmates to use when some of them had vandalized it in the past. "[Thevis] came highly recommended to us and there was no limit on how long we would let him use the telephone," Watkins explained. "According to the people we talked to, he is an honor-roll prisoner." The sheriff said that "high recommendation" had come from Thevis's attorney.[377]

Shortly after Thevis escaped, the FBI placed him on its top ten most-wanted list and focused significant resources on locating him. The new federal attention paid off, as on November 9, 1978, about a month after the ambush murder of Thevis's former business partner, Underhill, Thevis was apprehended at the Bloomfield State Bank in Bloomfield, Connecticut. Thevis was detained after trying to withdraw $33,000 from an account carrying the name Arbie J. Evans, the alias he gave bank officials who grew suspicious. At the time of his arrest, Thevis had attempted to alter his appearance by growing a beard and adding a toupee. In his car outside the bank, agents found and seized $560,000 in cash, and more than $1 million in jewels.[378]

When he was back in federal custody, U.S. attorney Virginia Dill McCarty in Indianapolis said the escape charges in Indiana would likely have to yield to the more serious pending charges elsewhere. The FBI also confirmed it had canceled its contract with the Floyd County Jail to assist in temporarily housing federal inmates.

On October 26, 1979, Thevis was sentenced to life in prison for his federal conviction on murder and conspiracy charges. U.S. District judge Harold Murphy also imposed an additional twenty-year sentence for racketeering.[379] Thevis died in prison on November 20, 2013, at the age of eighty-one.

7

1980-89

ONE MAN'S HATRED PLAYS OUT ACROSS INDIANA

Fugitive(s): Joseph Paul Franklin
Wanted For: January 12, 1980, murder, Indianapolis, Indiana
January 13, 1980, murder, Indianapolis, Indiana
May 28, 1980, attempted murder, Fort Wayne, Indiana
Captured: October 28, 1980, Lakeland, Florida

At the time of his crimes in Indiana, investigators didn't know they were looking at offences committed as part of a series of twenty-two murders stretching across the United States.

While the Indianapolis Police Department, like all big-city police agencies, was used to investigating homicides, two killings within twenty-four hours in January 1980 stood out as unusual from the start. The investigation would show both victims, twenty-two-year-old Lawrence E. Reese and nineteen-year-old Leo Thomas Watkins, were both assassinated by a sniper. The two men, both Black, were shot with a high-powered rifle from a gunman some distance away.

The Indianapolis murders were soon linked to a headline-making shooting on May 28, 1980, outside a Fort Wayne hotel where National Urban League president Vernon E. Jordan Jr. was critically wounded by a sniper's bullet.

By year's end, the pieces would start to come together with the October 28, 1980 arrest of Joseph Paul Franklin, a thirty-year-old Alabama native and virulent White supremacist. Franklin eventually confessed to as many as twenty-two murders and more than a dozen other injuries caused by his "hunting" of Black people and White people who he believed should not fraternize with one another.

In addition to Jordan, one of Franklin's other prominent victims was *Hustler* magazine publisher Larry Flynt, who was shot and permanently paralyzed on March 6, 1978, outside the Gwinnett County Courthouse in Lawrenceville, Georgia.

The cases in Indianapolis drew much less attention but were as troubling as could be. On Saturday night, January 12, Reese was shot as he stood in line to order food at about 11:00 p.m. at the Church's Chicken restaurant at 240 East Twenty-Second Street. He was shot in the back by a gunman who fired through the windows of the restaurant. "Four witnesses told police they heard what sounded like a gunshot, and saw Reese step forward and collapse," the *Indianapolis Star* reported.[380]

Indianapolis Police Department homicide detective Tom Minor said no motive had been determined for the shooting and that Reese, who lived nearby on College Avenue, was well known and well liked in the area.

The next day, police had a second murder of similar modus operandi. In the new case, Watkins was killed as he stood outside Mark's Quick-Pick Market at 2206 East Twenty-Fifth Street, just before 11:00 p.m. on January 13. "Police said Watkins was standing about five feet from the door when a shot was fired, striking him in his chest," the *Indianapolis Star* reported. "Watkins ran about 50 feet into the store, and then collapsed and died."[381]

Watkins and his father were at the store as part of their exterminating business. The bullet that struck Watkins was high-powered and passed through his body and lodged into the front of the store building. Indianapolis police were especially concerned about the sniper nature of the shootings and quickly formed a special investigative team of several detectives to determine who was responsible.

Award-winning *Indianapolis Star* columnist Thomas R. Keating took notice of the shootings, two of ten murders that took place in the first fifteen days of 1980. He noted police ballistics testing had shown that the same .30-caliber rifle was used to kill both Reese and Watkins. "Both victims were black men, near the same age, both were killed at about 11 p.m., at fast-food stores while standing in a well-lighted area," Indianapolis police captain Tim Foley told

Keating. "The stores are about two miles apart. But beyond that, the two men have no connection."[382]

Keating reported that homicide detectives had ruled out that Reese was shot by accident. "Now, and I hate to say this, but it looks like we have a nut who is killing indiscriminately," Foley said.[383]

Captain Foley couldn't have known it for certain, but he had placed his finger on what was happening with Joseph Paul Franklin and his ongoing reign of terror across several states.

FBI officials were being consulted, Foley said, to obtain a psychological profile of a suspect. "No one on the department can remember dealing with this kind of killer in Indianapolis," Foley noted.[384] The Indianapolis cases went cold quickly, however, and no arrests were made. It was not a case of Franklin changing his ways. It was simply a case of moving on from Indianapolis. He would resurface in the state soon enough.

On May 28, 1980, Vernon E. Jordan Jr., forty-four, was shot and critically wounded at about 2:00 a.m. as he walked from his car to the Marriott Hotel in Fort Wayne. Jordan had earlier addressed an audience of about five hundred meeting in Fort Wayne for the annual meeting of the National Urban League. Police confirmed Jordan was walking with a White woman at the time he was shot, but the woman was not injured.

Jordan's car was parked about fifty feet from the hotel door, police said. "As he exited the vehicle, walking around toward the rear of the car, the woman said he heard a shot fired and Mr. Jordan fell to the ground."[385]

News of Jordan's wounding was national news and was quickly referred to as an assassination attempt. President Jimmy Carter issued a statement from the White House, saying he was "shocked and saddened" by the attack and added, "Vernon is a valued leader and a personal friend. All of us are praying for his speedy and full recovery."[386]

Surgeons at Parkview Hospital in Fort Wayne reported Jordan was struck in the abdomen, with the bullet breaking into four fragments. He required more than four hours of surgery before his condition was stabilized. Fort Wayne police seemed reluctant to speculate that Jordan's shooting was race related, although FBI officials were quickly involved in the investigation. Urban League officials said they had received no threats on Jordan's life before the shooting.

As in the two Indianapolis shootings in January, police found evidence that a .30-caliber rifle was used to shoot Jordan. "The FBI is continuing to investigate the incident as a possible conspiracy, and authorities have reported there were three matted areas in the grass-covered knoll where the sniper may have waited for Jordan," the *Indianapolis Star* reported. "Police initially reported... the gunman may have waited at least 20 minutes for Jordan."[387]

FBI special agent Wayne G. Davis said the shooting was being considered "a deliberate act," but unlike President Carter and others, the FBI was stopping short of calling the shooting an assassination attempt. Carter made a hastily called visit to Jordan at the Fort Wayne hospital and said he was relieved Jordan had survived.[388]

There were no arrests in the Jordan shooting, and subsequent investigation showed that Franklin moved on from Fort Wayne to Cincinnati. On June 8, he shot and killed two Black teenage cousins who were walking along a street, though he said he had intended to shoot an interracial couple walking nearby.

On June 15, Franklin popped up again in Johnstown, Pennsylvania, where he shot and killed a young interracial couple. Ten days later, he killed two hitchhikers in Pocahontas County, West Virginia. Although his West Virginia victims were White, Franklin later told detectives he was angered that one of the women had said she previously dated a Black man. Before he was done, he killed two more Black men on August 20 in a park in Salt Lake City, Utah.

When he was finally apprehended, Franklin's arrest seemed almost uneventful for a man who had caused such havoc. Blood banks across the country had been given a description of Franklin, including distinctive tattoos, since he was known to sell plasma for money. In October 1980, a blood bank worker in Lakeland, Florida, recognized him, and police were notified and arrested Franklin. Convicted of several other killings (not including the Indiana ones), Franklin was eventually executed in a federal prison in Bonne Terre, Missouri, on November 20, 2013. He was sixty-three years old.

8

1990–99

HIDING IN PLAIN SIGHT

Fugitive(s): Mary Wright
Wanted For: May 10, 1969, escape, Indiana Women's Prison, Indianapolis, Indiana
Captured: July 24, 1991, Indianapolis, Indiana

On a spring night in 1969, Mary Wright was one of four women who scaled a fence at the Indiana Women's Prison in Indianapolis and went free. She stayed that way for twenty-two years.

Amazingly, Wright didn't go far, easily settling into the Near Eastside Indianapolis neighborhood where the prison is located, and eluded capture. It wasn't until July 24, 1991, with Wright pulled over for a burned-out brake light, that her odyssey finally ended.

"Prison fugitive Mary Wright knew her freedom was over the moment she saw the police car behind her," the Associated Press reported. "Now she fears she won't get her freedom back for a while."[389]

Now forty-one years old and the mother of six children (five of whom were born during her fugitive years), her case gained national attention because of her ability to hide undetected virtually within sight of the women's prison. She emphasized her clean record during the twenty-two years she was at large and posed for photographs for *Jet*, a national magazine. "I haven't been in any kind of trouble for the last 22 years, not even a traffic ticket until last night," Wright told a reporter. "There's no record of me in the last 22 years."[390]

On her last night of freedom, Wright borrowed a car from her daughter's boyfriend to pick up some tools to assemble bunk beds at home. As she drove to the hardware store, an Indiana State Police trooper pulled her over for the broken light. "I was scared to death. I knew he was going to find that warrant on me." She was right to be frightened, as the trooper placed her under arrest and lodged her in the Marion County Jail. New charges of escape and driving without a license were added.[391]

"I've been working and taking care of my children and living a normal life," Wright said. Explaining why she chose to never leave Indianapolis, she said, "I started having children, and it's kind of hard to take a family and just pick up and move away. If it wasn't for them, hard telling where I might be."[392]

Wright was originally sent to the women's prison on a charge of felony assault and battery for an incident that occurred on October 15, 1968, when she was a juvenile. At the time, Wright was housed at the Indiana Girls School in Plainfield on a charge of being a habitual truant from school. During a routine physical examination, she said a nurse poked her in the side, and because it hurt, she struck the sixty-three-year-old nurse.

Sentenced as an adult to the Indiana Women's Prison, Wright was convinced she had been treated unfairly. Strangely, although she was close to initial consideration for early release, she decided to join four other young women on May 10, 1969, in escaping. Eventually, the other three were rounded up, but Wright remained at large.

The night Wright escaped the prison was a raucous one. As police attempted to return two of the escapees that night, a small riot broke out. "About 15 inmates of the Indiana Women's Prison were subdued with chemical mace last night when they tried to attack two policemen returning two prisoners," the *Indianapolis Star* reported.[393]

"Before the disturbance was quelled, it involved about 50 inmates in three cottages," police said. "The inmates shouted obscenities and rushed the police officers. The original outbreak occurred in a residence cottage adjoining the security section on the second floor of the prison. The disturbance quickly spread to the building's ground floor residence cottage and to a third cottage in a nearby building. At least four small, unbarred windows were broken with hairbrushes and shoes."[394]

A total of seventy-four inmates lived in the three cottages, and as many as fifty of them joined in the riot, according to Valjean L. Dickinson, prison superintendent. Dickinson said the riot erupted because "the women are very protective of other members of their group. They may do things to each other in prison but they become angry when outsiders try to harm a member of the group. The women support inmates who try to go for the fence. They root for them like they would at a football game."[395]

In talking about her escape, Wright told a reporter she escaped because she felt her original sentence was unfair. Her time on the run, however, had been nerve-wracking. "I was sort of paranoid," she said. "I might be walking down the street, and they might get me for that [and] I had to stop living in fear. I thought they had forgotten about me until I done something wrong."[396]

As more years passed since she escaped, Wright's confidence grew. "For the first three or four years, I was really scared. For like a year, I changed my hairstyle and hair color. I wouldn't go out unless somebody else looked out the door to see if anyone was there. After about the fourth year, I put it out of mind. Otherwise, I would have been unable to lead a normal life, or the kids either."[397]

Wright was fortunate she had been a good citizen in the intervening years. In September, seven weeks after she was apprehended, Marion County judge Webster L. Brewer ordered her released. Brewster reduced her original one- to ten-year sentence down to seven weeks, plus the forty-four days she was jailed after arrested, and added one hundred hours of community service. Despite some limited criticism in the community for her release, Wright said she was grateful for the break Judge Brewer gave her. "I thought I would still be in there," she said. "The system worked against me last time and I had no idea that it would work for me this time."[398]

A TRIO OF DOPE HEADS DRIVEN TO ROB AND KILL

Fugitive(s): Benjamin Harold Brooks, Frederick James Treesh and Keisha Harth

Wanted For: August 10, 1994, bank robbery, Dyer, Indiana

August 12, 1994, bank robbery, Delavan, Wisconsin

August 16, 1994, bank robbery, Staples, Minnesota

August 1994, carjacking robberies, Brooklyn Park and St. Paul, Minnesota

August 24, 1994, carjacking, Sawyer, Michigan

August 25, 1994, murder, robbery, abduction, Livonia, Michigan
August 28, 1994, murder and robbery, Eastlake, Ohio
Captured: August 28, 1994, Euclid, Ohio

In a twisted variation on the traditional high school reunion, Frederick Tresh and his girlfriend Keisha Harth ran into an old school pal, Benjamin Brooks, in June 1994 outside of a Fort Wayne drug house and quickly renewed acquaintances. It was a reunion that would bring death and terror across the Midwest.

Treesh, thirty, and Harth, twenty-nine, met Brooks, twenty-seven, where they all went to get their latest fix. Crack cocaine was their drug of choice, and in 1994, it had all three of them in its grips. Eventually, Treesh and Brooks somehow convinced Harth's unsuspecting mother to allow the trio to move into her Waterloo, Indiana home. Restricted by their new living arrangements, however, the group decided on a plan of random violence to satiate their crippling drug addictions.

Wandering around Fort Wayne, Churubusco and Warsaw looking for victims to rob to gain new drug money, they finally arrived in Hammond in early August 1994. The trio were desperate drug addicts, and as the money ran out, with none of them working, they turned to robbery to find the resources they needed. Once in Lake County, they focused on the First Federal Savings Bank on Joliet Street in Dyer, Indiana (near the Illinois state border).

Treesh robbed the bank on August 10, 1994, as a lone gunman. His image was captured on a bank security camera as he entered the bank at about 12:20 p.m. and asked a teller about opening an account. "Suddenly, the man pulled out a blue metal gun and demanded cash," the *Times of Northwest Indiana* reported. "The teller gave the man an undisclosed amount of cash, and the man ran out the door onto Lake Street."[399]

A silent alarm was activated, but the man got away. Outside the bank in the getaway car were Brooks and Harth. "FBI agents and police officers converged on the bank, other police officers circled the area," the *Times* noted. "The Lake County police helicopter and dog were called out to aid the search, but to no avail."[400]

Harth later told investigators that Brooks hid on the floor of the truck under her legs and counted the money as Treesh drove away. Their total take was only $1,000.

The troubling and violent trio moved on through Illinois and into Wisconsin, where they robbed another bank at Delavan, Wisconsin, on

August 12. Four days later, they robbed a bank at Staples, Minnesota. Before fleeing Minnesota, the trio carjacked victims at both Brooklyn Park and St. Paul, before robbing and pistol-whipping a victim at Austin, Minnesota. By August 24, U.S. magistrate Judge Floyd Bolins approved federal warrants for Treesh and Brooks on multiple counts across several states. Because the crimes involved bank robberies and now stretched from Indiana north into Wisconsin and Minnesota, the FBI also joined the case.

Before police could catch up, however, another driver was carjacked near Sawyer, Michigan, and the case was quickly linked to the trio because one of the stolen vehicles from Minnesota was found nearby. Photographs of Treesh and Brooks were widely distributed to media throughout the Midwest, but it did nothing to slow them down.

On August 25, the Best Videos store in Livonia, Michigan, a western Detroit suburb, was robbed. During the robbery, the two brothers who own the store were shot just before the store's 11:00 p.m. closing time. Ghassen "Gus" Danno, thirty-nine, suffered multiple gunshot wounds and later died at the hospital. His brother, Frank Danno, thirty-six, was shot twice in the leg but survived.

For the first time, police acknowledged that they were looking for three suspects, not two, and that all three were from Indiana. Interestingly, however, the third suspect (Harth) was described as a male with no description available. "We know they have two handguns and a shotgun," said Livonia police lieutenant Pete Kunst. "They would be considered extremely dangerous, and we suggest if a citizen spots them, they call 911 and not do anything other than that."[401]

Apparently still in need of money—or at least enjoying their luck at armed robbery—Treesh and Brooks then robbed a motel, also in Livonia, the next day. Hours later, they forced their way into the home of Thomas and Janet Bushaw, two young parents in Livonia. Their fourteen-month-old child in a baby bed nearby was not harmed. The Bushaws were tied up and robbed of money and their car.

The next day, the Bushaws' car showed up outside the Vine Street Adult Bookstore in Eastlake, Ohio, a suburban Cleveland town along Lake Huron. Police said Treesh and Brooks both robbed the store and shot and wounded the store's security guard and a clerk. The guard, Henry Dupree, fifty-eight, died of his wound, and Louis Laver, forty-two, the clerk, was critically injured.

Following the robbery, a short chase ensued, and the trio was finally cornered and captured in Euclid, Ohio. It brought relief to many as

Lieutenant John Wiecek of the Eastlake, Ohio police said, "We got these animals off the street. Who knows what they could have done?"[402]

Drugs were assumed to be the driving force of the three's mad dash to infamy. As *Detroit Free Press* reporter Ginger Pullen offered, "It's hard to know what Brooks, Treesh and Harth had in mind when they left their Indiana homes last month in search of crack cocaine. But what is certain is that their search left an increasingly bloody trail."[403] Their final toll was staggering: two people dead, two injured critically by gunfire and more than thirty beaten and robbed across five states in three weeks.

Once in custody, Treesh talked freely with a reporter from the *Cleveland Plain Dealer*, blaming his insatiable drug habit for his crimes. Treesh spoke to the newspaper "in hopes of persuading youths to stay off drugs," the *Plain Dealer* reported. "Don't use drugs," Treesh advised from an Ohio jail. "I mean that from the bottom of my heart. Everyone knows when you do cocaine you get a numb feeling. So you don't care. You have no feelings for anyone. If one kid reads this, I hope they realize how truly serious this is."[404]

Treesh said his common-law wife, Harth, was not involved in the robberies and should not be charged. "We never intended to kill," Treesh said. "I wish it never had happened. It was the drugs. You have to understand, we were on cocaine. When you're on cocaine, you want more and more."[405]

In September 1994, murder and attempted murder charges (among others) were added for Treesh and Brooks in Michigan, as they were already under indictment for murder and robbery in Ohio. Trial for the murder of the security guard at the adult bookstore in Ohio got underway in February 1995, with Treesh claiming the shooting was accidental. Found guilty on the charges, Treesh was sentenced to death by a Lake County, Ohio judge.[406]

Following the outcome of Treesh's trial, Brooks changed his plea to guilty to a charge of murder and four other charges. The same judge who sentenced Treesh to die sentenced Brooks to fifty-six years in prison.[407]

On October 27, 1995, Treesh and Brooks were both convicted of bank robbery charges stemming from the Dyer, Indiana robbery, but neither would see the inside of an Indiana jail, as they were confined already in Ohio.

For her part in the crime spree, Harth was sentenced to seven to twenty-five years in prison after entering a guilty plea in Ohio to charges of complicity to commit aggravated murder, robbery and fleeing police.[408]

In February 2013, Ohio's parole board denied a clemency request for Treesh and allowed his death sentence to proceed.[409] He was executed by the State of Ohio on March 6, 2013.[410]

A FUGITIVE WITH AMNESIA

Fugitive(s): Carl Brodnik Jr., also known as Pat Brown
Wanted For: July 1994, theft via embezzlement, Indianapolis, Indiana
Captured: April 12, 1998, Jackson Hole, Wyoming

When Carl Brodnik Jr. disappeared without explanation on a July day in 1994, he left a mystery about why he left and where he was. It was a mystery Brodnik said existed even to himself.

Last seen leaving for work, Brodnik, forty-nine, was first reported missing on July 8, 1994, by his wife, Pat. He left her behind with two sons, ages twenty-one and seventeen, but not before withdrawing $1,000 from a bank account and walking off with the proceeds of a second mortgage taken on his Indianapolis home.

Clues to his whereabouts quickly dried up. His car was located in an airport parking lot in St. Louis just days after he went missing, and one of his credit cards was used a few days later in Denver. From there, the trail went cold.

Unknown to Mrs. Brodnik and her family after reporting him missing, on July 19, 1984, a hitchhiker outside Cheyenne, Wyoming, stumbled upon a confused man. The man was lying in a ditch near Interstate 80, bruised, confused and carrying twenty-three cents in his pocket. He carried no identification and said he had no idea who he was.

Taken to a Cheyenne homeless shelter, the man said he could remember the name "Pat" and added "Brown" as a last name, since the desk in front of him was the color brown. Moving on, "Brown began piecing a new life together, while trying to rediscover the life he had lost," *Indianapolis Star* reporter Bill Theobald wrote. "He ended up in Jackson [Wyoming] because he couldn't get work in Cheyenne without a Social Security number."[411]

The mystery man who said he couldn't remember his past was soon hired by the *Jackson Hole Guide*, a weekly newspaper, to work in the pressroom. Parishioners at Our Lady of the Mountains Catholic Church befriended him and believed his made-up story that he had left behind a messy divorce and asked no further questions.

"Brown" eventually also made up a Social Security number to get a job. His bosses at the newspaper office notified him that the Social Security Administration said his number did not match up, and Brown began elaborating that he had no memory of his past and was suffering from amnesia. Among those who took in Brown's story was Curtis Hubbard, the editor of the *Jackson Hole Guide*, who eventually wrote stories about the mysterious man who said he didn't know his past.

With the help of his new friends—including a paralegal at his church and with intervention from U.S. representative Barbara Cubin, Wyoming's sole member of the lower house—a new Social Security number was created, and Pat Brown moved on. However, those around Brown suggested he try to ask for help uncovering a past he could not remember. One friend thought contacting the television program *Unsolved Mysteries*, hosted by actor Robert Stack, was a good idea. It turned out to be a bad idea.

For reasons that perhaps only he understood, Brown decided to go ahead and participate with taping a segment for *Unsolved Mysteries*, which aired nationally on CBS on April 10, 1998. By Easter Sunday, 1998, the mystery of Pat Brown was solved within minutes of a series of telephone calls to the show from some Indianapolis viewers.

They quickly recognized Pat Brown was actually Carl Brodnik Jr., who went missing in July 1994 and hadn't been heard from in almost four years. One of his childhood friends from the Haughville neighborhood told a reporter she had to convince a skeptical telephone operator at *Unsolved Mysteries* that she knew who the man was, but soon, Brodnik's wife and children were also informed of the TV segment.[412]

Brown soon called his wife, Pat, back in Indianapolis for a long-awaited reunion. A lot had changed in the intervening years—Pat Brodnik sought and was granted a divorce from her missing husband in 1995, the same year his elderly father passed away. His mother died in 1996, both parents dying before knowing what had happened to their lost son.[413]

A jubilant Carl Brodnik was pictured by the *Jackson Hole Guide* in a photograph moved across newswires showing him talking on the phone with his long-lost wife, Pat. "How do you capture three and a half years of a nightmare," Pat told one reporter. "It's hard to express how happy we are."[414]

Apparently used to referring to her husband in the past tense, Pat Brodnik corrected herself when talking about a planned reunion. "He was, er, is a wonderful man," she said.[415]

Still holding to his story that he had no memory of his Indiana past, Carl Brodnik told *Indianapolis News* reporter Eric Schoch, "It's like a tornado inside your head. It's just going around so fast you don't really have time to think or even feel. It's more numb than anything else." Brodnik said the family would "take it slow" regarding a reunion, given that he was asserting he had no memory of them. "It's real hard living without a past," he said. "It's even harder living without a Social Security number."[416]

A few days in the media spotlight, however, and Brodnik's elaborate story began to unwind as the Marion County Sheriff's Department confirmed that it was holding fugitive warrants for Brodnik's arrest for alleged embezzlement occurring in 1994, just before he went missing.

"Maybe he does have amnesia, but I'm not that naïve," said Detective Donald Lee. "It's just too coincidental."[417] Michael Hoak, deputy chief in charge of investigations for the sheriff's department remarked, "C'mon, I've been a cop for 24 years, I'm skeptical. You have to prove it to me."[418]

Marion County authorities moved quickly to extradite Brodnik to Indiana on a fugitive warrant for six counts of theft. Informed of the criminal issues back in Indiana, Brodnik turned himself in to police in Wyoming, but was still holding on to his amnesia tale, while mostly avoiding reporters he had talked to just twenty-four hours earlier.

His friends at the *Jackson Hole Guide* found themselves in a tough spot, needing to report on the details of the "Pat Brown" story but also wanting to remain sympathetic to their friend and employee. In fact, just as the amnesia story was breaking, the newspaper had decided to promote Brodnik from a pressroom job to circulation manager.

By its April 22, 1998 weekly edition, the *Jackson Hole Guide* had at least begun to suggest there were serious doubts about Brodnik's story. Reporter Thomas Dewell noted, "Amnesia is a familiar plot device" in television dramas. "For Jackson resident, Carl Brodnik, Jr. amnesia is the malady that holds together the tale of how he turned up in Wyoming, not knowing who he was and found his way to this valley where labor was in such demand that a man could get a job without a valid Social Security card."[419]

Dewell noted, while ABC's primetime news program *20/20* was coming to Wyoming to tell the story of Pat Brown, "Without the cover of amnesia, Brodnik [appears] as a warped and perhaps pathetic criminal who fled Indianapolis, following an embezzlement crime and concocted an elaborate amnesia cover-up."[420]

Brodnik declined to talk to reporters and was silent as he was booked at the Teton County Jail. Bond was set and paid for $3,500, and he walked free. Asked by one of his jailors if he was Carl Brodnik, he replied, "That's what they've told me."[421]

On April 30, 1998, Brodnik appeared at the City-County Building in downtown Indianapolis with his wife, Pat, on his arm to formally surrender to the charges pending against him. The six theft charges were related to his work as an accountant for an Indianapolis public relations firm (that later folded) and totaled nearly $24,000. Prosecutors said they found checks of more than $16,000 made out directly to Brodnik and another $7,498 in checks made payable to remodeling firms that completed work on his Indianapolis home.[422]

In July, reporter Mark Huffman at the *Jackson Hole News* poked major holes in Brodnik's amnesia story by uncovering that he had used the name Carl Brodnik Jr. at two missions in Wyoming days after he stated he had no memory of who he was. An investigator with the Jackson, Wyoming police uncovered the slipups the so-called amnesia victim made and noted, "You can draw the conclusions you want. It appears maybe his amnesia was—sporadic."[423]

With the amnesia story basically shredded by facts that could not be dismissed, the *Jackson Hole Guide* finally dropped Brodnik's name from its masthead as one of the circulation staff with its August 5, 1998 edition. In October 1998, *20/20* ran its segment including heartwarming photos of Brodnik reunited with his long-lost wife and sons. The matter came to an end on February 25, 1999, when Brodnik pleaded guilty to one count of theft in an agreement reached with prosecutors. Still maintaining that he had no memory of the crime, he nonetheless agreed to take a guilty plea, one that could land him jail time, and would require him to repay $23,618 stolen in 1994.[424]

The previously talkative Brodnik slipped in and out of the courtroom without answering any reporters' questions shouted at him. He was equally quiet on May 14, 1999, after Marion County judge Charles A. Wiles sentenced Brodnik to a year and a half on probation, one hundred days of home detention and two hundred hours of community service.

One of the partners in the now defunct PR firm was present in court to claim the funds, while a lawyer representing a local bank was also present. The bank had lent the PR firm funds between 1994 and 1996, and not all of them had been repaid. In addition, an IRS representative had notified the court that the PR firm had an unpaid tax bill that still needed to be settled. The judge said he would review who should receive the restitution funds paid by Brodnik through his wife, Pat.[425]

Brodnik eventually went back to Wyoming and was rehired to work in the circulation department for the *Jackson Hole Guide*. In June 2004, the newspaper's business pages reported Brodnik was the new proprietor of a local coffee shop, the Hole Bean. Under a large photograph of a smiling Brodnik, he said he bought the shop because "it's fun meeting and greeting people" and added, "I like to bake and saw the place was for sale" and planned to offer his own baked creations to customers.[426]

END OF THE ROAD FOR "TACO" BOWMAN

Fugitive(s): Harry Joseph "Taco" Bowman
Wanted For: January 28, 1995, murder, Gary, Indiana
Captured: June 7, 1999, Sterling Heights, Michigan

"Taco" Bowman, as he was known among the Outlaws motorcycle gang that he headed for many years, was a wanted man in 1999 for many things—including a 1995 Indiana murder.

The Indiana murder, committed on January 28, 1995, left Donald "Big Don" Fogg, thirty-four, of Lake Station, Indiana, dead. It was a case that made headlines and then just as quickly went cold for years. It wasn't until March 1998 that the FBI named Bowman as a suspect in the Fogg killing. By then, Bowman was already listed as one of the nation's Ten Most Wanted Criminals.[427]

Bowman remained free until arrested by FBI agents in Sterling Heights, Michigan, on June 7, 1999. He reportedly surrendered after a "brief, but quiet standoff," when FBI agents surrounded his house.[428] Authorities held an indictment charging Bowman with murder, bombing, drug dealing, racketeering and conspiracy. The *Detroit Free-Press* noted that the indictment also included charges related to plots to kill police officers and members of the Hell's Angels, as well as plans to blow up the Warlock's clubhouse and a clubhouse of Hell's Henchmen.[429]

"The indictment identifies Bowman as the international president of the Outlaws Motorcycle Club and paints a picture of a ruthless leader responsible for two slayings and blasts at rival gang hangouts," said the *Tampa Tribune*.[430]

The nondescript suburban neighborhood where Bowman lived was one that perhaps would surprise others. It held all of the signs of a normal, middle-class neighborhood, but inside was a man living on borrowed time since his case was profiled on the FOX program *America's Most Wanted*. One of Bowman's neighbors remarked, "We always thought they were a little rough, but they mow their lawn and they plant flowers. I wouldn't have guessed anything was going on over there."[431]

In addition to the Indiana slaying, Bowman was accused of the 1982 murder of club member Arthur "Good Old Speed" Vincent and the 1991 murder of Raymond Chaffin, the president of a rival club, the Warlocks.

The Outlaws, an often violent and powerful gang, reportedly had clubs in more than thirty U.S. cities and twenty chapters in other countries around the world. Over time, Bowman had become the leader of the entire operation that the FBI said funded its efforts through drug dealing, robbery, burglary, gun dealing, prostitution, intimidation and blackmail.

In northwest Indiana, Bowman's name soon became familiar after the spectacle of Fogg's funeral played out in Portage over two days in February 1995. Just as Fogg was to be laid to rest, the FBI and the Bureau of Alcohol, Tobacco and Firearms (ATF) formally announced it had entered the investigation of his death.

Fogg was found dead in a city park along Industrial Boulevard in Gary. Fogg, suffering three gunshot wounds to the back of his head, was found slumped over inside a pick-up truck. A .45-caliber pistol found in his pocket had not been fired. Police reportedly also found the bloody clothing of a member of the rival Hell's Angels motorcycle club in Fogg's vehicle, which they believe was tied to a September 1994 murder.

"Federal authorities identified Fogg as the [local Outlaw] chapter's 'enforcer,' a sort of sergeant at arms who is responsible for keeping order within the chapter and doling out punishment by the chapter president," reported Mark Kiesling of the *Times of Northwest Indiana.* Because of the alleged connection between Fogg and the Hell's Angels murder, police were unsure if his own slaying was the result of a rival gang's retribution or not. "We know that these two gangs are at war, but there is no way Don Fogg was going to allow a Hell's Angel to climb into his pickup truck with him," Gary police detective Anthony Titus said.[432]

The Engel Funeral Home in Portage was engaged to conduct the funeral and burial for Fogg, with the *Times of Northwest Indiana* noting, "It will be a funeral like no other ever held" at the funeral home. Funeral director Vernon Engel said he took charge of Fogg's services because he had known Fogg's family for many years. "I have known this family since this boy was in Sunday school," he said. "I led both him and his mother to the Lord many years ago." Engel reported that members of the Outlaws motorcycle club had been "very easy to work with" and all had acted like "gentlemen and ladies."[433]

No cameras were going to be allowed inside the funeral home, Engel said, even though Fogg's death was attracting some media attention. The funeral itself drew more than two hundred family and friends, including an elaborate and lengthy motorcade of motorcycles following the hearse from the funeral home to McCool Cemetery in Portage.

Kiesling reported, "There was enough leather inside the Engel Funeral Home to outfit a small herd of cattle as bikers crowded shoulder to shoulder, packing the room in which Fogg lay surrounded by a sea of floral tributes, many of which carried the club insignia and slogans." Randy M. "Mad" Yager, president of the Gary Outlaws chapter, spoke at the funeral, noting, "We're here to bury a brother. You'll see that things are done properly, that they are done with respect."[434]

Interestingly, the earlier story about Fogg's funeral in the *Times of Northwest Indiana* highlighted the many Outlaws motorcycle club members who attended the funeral from around the nation. One mention noted, "Taco was down from Detroit" at the funeral—the same Harry Joseph "Taco" Bowman charged three years later with Fogg's murder.[435]

For his part, "Taco" Bowman was found guilty on eight separate counts (including two murders) at Tampa, Florida, in April 2001.[436] He later received two life sentences. He was never tried or convicted of the Fogg murder. He died in a federal prison in Butner, North Carolina, on March 3, 2019, at the age of sixty-nine. More than two thousand people attended Bowman's funeral in Dayton, Ohio, including more than 1,200 bikers.[437]

NOTES

Introduction

1. Tom Reynolds, *I Hate Myself and Want to Die: The 52 Most Depressing Songs You've Ever Heard* (New York: Hyperion Books, 2006).
2. David Sedaris, *Children Playing Before a Statue of Hercules* (Sydney, Australia: Simon & Schuster UK, 2005).

Chapter 1

3. *Indianapolis Star*, April 12, 1920.
4. *Indianapolis News*, May 17, 1920.
5. *Indianapolis Star*, July 5, 1920.
6. *Indianapolis News*, August 30, 1920.
7. *Indianapolis Star*, June 8, 1921.
8. *Indianapolis News*, December 12, 1921; Associated Press, December 26, 1921.
9. *Indianapolis Star*, January 22, 1922.
10. Ibid.
11. *Indianapolis News*, Febuary 6, 1922.
12. *Daily Oklahoman* (Oklahoma City, OK), January 9, 1925.
13. Ibid.
14. *Indianapolis News*, April 1, 1926.

15. Associated Press, April 2 and 6, 1926.
16. International News Service, October 3, 1927.
17. United Press, August 28, 1928.
18. *Princeton Daily Clarion*, September 26, 1928.
19. Associated Press, November 19 and 23, 1928.
20. *Indianapolis Star*, September 14, 1928; July 3, 1930.
21. Associated Press, January 23, 1931.
22. *Indianapolis Star*, January 26, 1931.
23. International News Service, January 12, 1933; January 2–3, 1936; *Vincennes Sun-Commercial*, November 21, 1975.
24. *Los Angeles Times*, May 14, 1935.
25. *Indianapolis Star*, March 3, 1927.
26. *Hammond Times*, April 6, 1927.
27. *Gary Evening Times*, April 7, 1927.
28. Bill Demain, "Smooth Operator: How Con Man 'Count' Victor Lustig Sold the Eiffel Tower—Twice," Mental Floss, August 21, 2020, http://mentalfloss.com.
29. *Boston Globe*, January 11, 1930.
30. Ibid., February 9, 1932.
31. *Hammond Times*, December 16, 1930.
32. *St. Louis Post-Dispatch*, July 19, 1931.
33. *Hammond Times*, May 14, 1935.
34. *New York Daily News*, May 14, 1935.
35. Associated Press, September 2, 1935.
36. *New York Daily News*, September 2, 1935.
37. *Hammond Times*, December 10, 1935.
38. *Des Moines Register*, October 26, 1947.
39. *Indianapolis News*, May 18, 1926.
40. Ibid.
41. Ibid.
42. Ibid.
43. Ibid.
44. Deborah B. Markinsohn, *The Encyclopedia of Indianapolis*, eds. D.J. Brodenhamer and R.G. Barrows (Bloomington: Indiana University Press, 1994), 652–53.
45. *Indianapolis News*, May 18, 1926.
46. *Indianapolis Star*, May 21, 1926.
47. *Chicago Tribune*, October 28, 1926; October 13, 1927.
48. *Indianapolis Star*, July 20, 1928; *San Francisco Examiner*, July 19, 1928.

49. *Indianapolis Star*, August 4, 1928.
50. Ibid., August 18, 1928.
51. Ibid., March 14, 1929.
52. Ibid.
53. Ibid., March 20, 1929; March 25, 1929; March 7, 1944.
54. *South Bend Tribune*, January 24, 1927.
55. Ibid., September 16, 1926.
56. Associated Press, September 23, 1926.
57. *South Bend Tribune*, March 29, 1926
58. Ibid., January 24, 1927.
59. Ibid.
60. Ibid., February 17–18, 1927.
61. United Press, April 10, 1928.
62. *Lafayette Journal & Courier*, January 4, 1928.
63. Ibid., December 23, 1927.
64. Ibid., January 12, 1928.
65. Ibid., February 3, 1928.
66. Ibid., February 8, 1928.
67. Ibid.
68. Ibid., February 9, 1928.
69. Ibid.
70. Ibid., February 10, 1928.
71. Ibid., February 11, 1928.
72. Ibid., February 16, 1928.
73. Ibid.
74. Ibid., February 17, 1928.
75. Ibid., May 21, 1928.
76. Ibid.
77. Ibid., May 22, 1928.
78. Ibid., June 9, 1928.
79. *Albuquerque Journal*, August 28, 1931.
80. Ibid., September 2, 1931.
81. *Lafayette Journal & Courier*, September 28; October 16, 1931.
82. Ibid., January 9, 1932.

Chapter 2

83. *Orlando Sentinel*, April 6, 1930.

84. *Orlando Evening Star*, April 4, 1930.
85. *Indianapolis Star*, March 13, 1930.
86. Ibid.
87. Ibid., March 14, 1930.
88. *Indianapolis News*, March 15, 1930.
89. *Indianapolis Star*, March 25, 1930.
90. Ibid.
91. Ibid.
92. Ibid., April 13, 1930.
93. Ibid.
94. Ibid., January 31, 1931.
95. Ibid., March 25, 1930.
96. *Indianapolis News*, February 7, 1933.
97. Ibid.
98. Ibid.
99. Ibid.
100. *Indianapolis Star*, November 5, 1935.
101. *Indianapolis News*, February 7, 1933.
102. Ibid.
103. Ibid., February 7, 1933.
104. *Louisville Courier-Journal*, March 21; April 23–24, 1933.
105. *Indianapolis Star*, November 5, 1935.
106. Ibid., April 30, 1933.
107. Associated Press, August 22, 1934.
108. International News Service, September 10, 1934.
109. *Indianapolis Star*, November 5, 1935.
110. Associated Press, November 10, 1934.
111. *Indianapolis Star*, June 13, 1953; *Indianapolis News*, June 12, 1953.
112. *Indianapolis Star*, May 2, 1933.
113. *Indianapolis Star*, December 20, 1933; Associated Press, December 20–21, 1933.
114. *Indianapolis Star*, December 21, 1933.
115. Ibid., October 13, 1933.
116. Christopher Goodwin, "America's Own Robin Hood, the Dillinger Legend," *Sunday Times*, June 29, 2009.
117. *Indianapolis Star*, October 24, 1933.
118. *Hammond Times*, January 16, 1934.
119. International News Service, January 26, 1934.
120. *South Bend Tribune*, July 1, 1934.

121. Associated Press, October 17, 1934.
122. *Indianapolis News*, October 31, 1938.
123. Ibid.
124. Ibid.
125. Ibid.
126. *Indianapolis News*, November 1, 1938; *Indianapolis Star*, November 2, 1938.
127. *Indianapolis News*, November 2, 1938.
128. *Indianapolis Star*, November 2, 1938.
129. *Franklin County Tribune* (Union, MO), November 25, 1938.
130. *New York Daily News*, May 12, 1939.
131. *South Bend Tribune*, April 29, 1939.
132. Ibid., April 29, 1939; June 24, 1939.
133. Ibid., April 29, 1939.
134. Ibid.
135. Ibid.
136. Ibid.
137. Ibid., May 1, 1938.
138. Ibid.
139. Ibid., June 24, 1938.
140. Ibid., May 11, 1939.

Chapter 3

141. *Odessa* (TX) *American*, April 8, 1940.
142. *Elwood Call Leader*, November 6, 1930.
143. *Elwood Call Leader*, August 3, 1931.
144. *Pittsburgh Sun-Telegraph*, October 20, 1933.
145. *Elwood Call Leader*, October 20, 1933.
146. *Pittsburgh Sun-Telegraph*, December 12, 1933.
147. Associated Press, January 29, 1934.
148. *Miami News*, February 8, 1934.
149. Associated Press, March 7, 1934.
150. Associated Press, August 11, 1934.
151. Ibid.
152. *New York Daily News*, August 12, 1934.
153. *Miami News*, March 4, 1936; March 6, 1936.
154. *Indianapolis Star*, June 2, 1937.

155. Ibid.
156. United Press, October 7, 1938; *Indianapolis Star*, October 7, 1938.
157. *New York Daily News*, May 17, 1942.
158. *Elwood Call Leader*, April 30, 1940.
159. Associated Press, June 4, 1940.
160. *Elwood Call Leader*, June 5, 1940.
161. Ibid.
162. Associated Press, November 12, 1940.
163. Ibid., March 18, 1940.
164. Ibid., April 23, 1940.
165. Thomas C. Stone, Elwood's Gun Girl. Elwood Genealogy Society: Elwood, Indiana, 2013.
166. *Lafayette Journal & Courier*, July 7, 1942.
167. Ibid.
168. Ibid.
169. Ibid.
170. Associated Press, August 21, 1942.
171. *Lafayette Journal & Courier*, August 17, 1942.
172. *Reno Gazette-Journal*, August 21, 1942.
173. Ibid.
174. United Press, October 1, 1942.
175. *Lafayette Journal & Courier*, September 27, 1944.
176. Associated Press, September 29, 1944.
177. *Los Angeles Times*, June 3, 1943.
178. Ibid., June 4, 1943.
179. Ibid., June 3, 1943.
180. United Press, June 7, 1943; Associated Press, June 7, 1943.
181. International News Service, June 26, 1943.
182. *Indianapolis News*, May 20, 1919.
183. Associated Press, June 28, 1943.
184. *Los Angeles Times*, June 30, 1943.
185. Ibid., August 13, 1943.

Chapter 4

186. *Logansport Pharos-Tribune*, June 6, 1953.
187. Ibid., June 8, 1953.
188. *St. Louis Globe-Democrat*, August 23, 1953.

189. Associated Press, July 17, 1953.
190. *St. Louis Globe-Democrat*, August 23, 1953.
191. *Logansport Pharos-Tribune*, August 24, 1953.
192. Ibid.
193. Associated Press, November 29, 1953.
194. *Arizona Republic*, February 19, 1954.
195. Ibid.
196. Ibid.
197. *Indianapolis News*, May 27, 1940.
198. *Indianapolis Star*, June 1, 1940.
199. Ibid., May 28, 1940.
200. Ibid., September 13, 1940.
201. Ibid.
202. *Indianapolis News*, May 28, 1940.
203. *Indianapolis Star*, May 29, 1940.
204. Ibid., June 24, 1940.
205. Ibid.
206. Ibid.
207. Ibid., July 23, 1940.
208. Ibid., April 21, 1941.
209. Ibid.
210. Ibid., July 8, 1941.
211. Associated Press, February 10, 1956.
212. Ibid.
213. *San Francisco Examiner*, February 10, 1956.
214. Ibid.
215. Associated Press, February 10, 1956.
216. *Irvin v. Dowd*, 366 U.S. 717, opinion of the U.S. Supreme Court, decided June 5, 1961, https://en.wikisource.org.
217. *St. Louis Post-Dispatch*, October 4, 1958.
218. *Indianapolis Star*, October 4, 1958.
219. Ibid., April 11, 1957; Associated Press, April 11, 1957.
220. Associated Press, June 25, 1958.
221. *St. Louis Post-Dispatch*, April 13, 1959.
222. Ibid., May 18, 1959.
223. Associated Press, May 18, 1959.
224. Associated Press, February 19, 1959.
225. *Decatur* (IL) *Daily Review*, February 19, 1959.
226. Ibid.

227. Ibid.
228. *Indianapolis Star*, September 11, 1960.
229. Ibid., September 13, 1960.
230. Ibid., September 11, 1960.
231. Ibid.
232. King Features Syndicate, June 14, 1960.
233. Associated Press, December 31, 1960; *Indianapolis Star*, April 14, 1961.
234. Associated Press, April 21, 1960.
235. *Indianapolis News*, September 30, 1963.
236. Ibid., April 20, 1938.
237. Ibid., October 5, 1938.
238. Ibid., March 23, 1937.
239. Ibid., December 20, 1937.
240. Ibid., January 21, 1939; *Indianapolis Star*, January 22, 1939.

Chapter 5

241. United Press International, June 6, 1960.
242. *South Bend Tribune*, December 5, 1959.
243. *Logansport Press*, January 30, 1960.
244. Ibid.
245. *Logansport Press*, February 2, 1960.
246. *Indianapolis Star*, August 18, 1960.
247. *Salina* (KS) *Journal*, February 13, 1962.
248. *Indianapolis Star*, December 14, 1961.
249. Ibid.
250. Ibid.
251. Ibid.
252. Ibid.
253. Ibid., December 15, 1961.
254. Ibid., December 13, 1963.
255. *Columbus Evening Republican*, July 12, 1962.
256. Ibid.
257. *Monongahela* (PA) *Daily Republican*, August 14, 1962.
258. *Columbus Evening Republican*, July 12, 1962.
259. Ibid.
260. *Indianapolis Star*, December 10, 1962.
261. *Hartford* (CT) *Courant*, December 19, 1962.

262. Ibid.
263. *Noblesville Ledger*, April 12, 1963.
264. Ibid., April 20, 1963.
265. *Indianapolis Star*, April 20, 1963; *Indianapolis News*, April 19, 1963.
266. *Indianapolis Star*, April 20, 1963.
267. Michael Newton, *Silent Rage: Inside the Mind of a Serial Killer* (Sanger, CA: Write Thought, Inc., 2014).
268. Associated Press, January 17, 1975.
269. *Chicago Daily Herald*, November 18, 1974.
270. *Wheeling* (IL) *Herald*, January 17, 1975.
271. *Chicago Tribune*, February 23, 1977.
272. Ibid.
273. Ibid.
274. Ibid.
275. *Hammond Times*, March 21, 1987.
276. Associated Press, April 22, 1941.
277. Ibid.
278. Ibid.
279. *Chicago Tribune*, April 22, 1941.
280. Associated Press, July 31, 1941.
281. United Press, December 2, 1941.
282. *Terre Haute Tribune*, September 6, 1960.
283. *Arizona Daily Star* (Tucson, AZ), March 25, 1961.
284. *Tucson* (AZ) *Daily Citizen*, March 29, 1961.
285. Ibid.
286. Arizona Republic (Phoenix, AZ), December 7, 1962.
287. Associated Press, December 8, 1962.
288. *Springfield* (MO) *News-Leader*, November 27, 1962.
289. *Arizona Daily Star*, December 11, 1962.
290. *Tucson Daily Citizen*, December 13, 1962.
291. Ibid.
292. Ibid.
293. *Arizona Republic*, January 1, 1963.
294. *Indianapolis News*, May 23, 1966.
295. Ibid.
296. Ibid.
297. Associated Press, May 24, 1966.
298. Ibid.
299. Ibid.

300. Ibid.
301. *Indianapolis Star*, May 25, 1966.
302. Ibid.
303. *Indianapolis News*, April 14, 1967; August 23, 1973.
304. Associated Press, June 30, 1967; December 11, 1969.
305. *South Bend Tribune*, August 4, 1967.
306. Ibid., August 5, 1967.
307. *Lincoln* (NE) *Evening Journal*, August 10, 1967.
308. Ibid., January 16, 1968.
309. Ibid., February 15, 1968.
310. Ibid., July 31, 1968.
311. Ibid., July 29–31, 1969.
312. Ibid., July 17, 1971.
313. Associated Press, August 11, 1983.
314. United Press International, October 29, 1983.
315. Associated Press, March 24, 1984; October 3, 1984.
316. *Des Moines Register*, April 23, 1985.
317. United Press International, March 20, 1969.
318. FBI Most Wanted poster, issued February 25, 1969.
319. United Press International, March 20, 1969.
320. Associated Press, July 12, 1968.
321. United Press International, March 20, 1969.
322. *Chicago Tribune*, March 30, 1969.
323. *South Bend Tribune*, November 27, 1968
324. Ibid.
325. Ibid.
326. Ibid.
327. Ibid., December 12 ,1969.

Chapter 6

328. *Greenfield Daily Reporter*, March 18, 1970.
329. *Indianapolis Star*, March 19, 1970.
330. Associated Press, December 20, 1979.
331. Ibid., December 20, 1979.
332. *Indianapolis News*, May 12, 1983.
333. *Indianapolis Star*, May 12, 1983.
334. Ibid., May 12, 1983.

335. Ibid.
336. *Indianapolis Star*, September 26, 1984.
337. *Hammond Times*, March 14, 1972.
338. Associated Press, October 23, 2007.
339. *Hammond Times*, March 4, 1970.
340. Ibid.
341. Ibid.
342. Ibid., March 5, 1970.
343. Ibid.
344. Ibid., March 6, 1970.
345. Associated Press, March 10, 1970.
346. *Hammond Times*, June 11, 1970.
347. Ibid., September 20, 1970.
348. Ibid., September 25, 1970; Associated Press, October 2, 1970.
349. *Nashville Tennessean*, October 17, 2007.
350. Ibid.
351. *Ashland* (KY) *Daily Independent*, October 24, 2007.
352. United Press International, June 24, 1982.
353. Associated Press, June 25, 1982.
354. *Indianapolis Star*, April 10, 1972.
355. United Press International, June 24, 1982.
356. Associated Press, June 25, 1982.
357. United Press International, November 17, 1982.
358. Associated Press, November 18, 1982.
359. *Chicago Tribune*, October 25, 1986.
360. *Times of Northwest Indiana*, October 25, 1986.
361. *Franklin Daily Journal*, January 21, 1974.
362. Ibid., January 22, 1974.
363. Ibid., January 28, 1974.
364. Ibid.
365. *Indianapolis News*, November 18, 1974.
366. Ibid.
367. Ibid.
368. Ibid.
369. *Indianapolis Star*, November 28, 1974.
370. Ibid., December 19, 1974; June 26, 1976.
371. *Indianapolis News*, January 14, 1977.
372. *New York Daily News*, February 11, 1988.
373. *Atlanta Constitution*, October 26, 1978.

374. Associated Press, November 10, 1978.
375. *Louisville Courier-Journal*, April 30, 1978.
376. Ibid.
377. Ibid.
378. Associated Press, November 10, 1978; *Hartford Courant*, November 10, 1978.
379. Associated Press, October 27, 1978.

Chapter 7

380. *Indianapolis Star*, January 12, 1980; January 14, 1980.
381. Ibid., January 15, 1980.
382. Ibid., January 16, 1980.
383. Ibid.
384. Ibid.
385. *Indianapolis News*, May 29, 1980.
386. Ibid.
387. *Indianapolis Star*, June 1, 1980.
388. Ibid.

Chapter 8

389. Associated Press, July 26, 1991.
390. Ibid.
391. Ibid.
392. *Franklin Daily Journal*, July 26, 1991.
393. *Indianapolis Star*, May 11, 1969.
394. Ibid.
395. Ibid.
396. *Franklin Daily Journal*, July 26, 1991.
397. *Indianapolis Star*, November 28, 1991.
398. Ibid.
399. *Times of Northwest Indiana*, August 11, 1994.
400. Ibid.
401. *Detroit Free-Press*, August 27, 1994.
402. Ibid., August 29, 1994.
403. Ibid.

404. Associated Press, August 31, 1994.
405. Ibid.
406. Associated Press, March 4, 1995.
407. Ibid., March 30, 1995.
408. Ibid., February 9, 1995.
409. *Dayton* (OH) *Daily News*, February 9, 2013.
410. Associated Press, March 7, 2013.
411. *Indianapolis Star*, April 12, 1998.
412. Ibid.
413. Ibid., January 10, 1995; June 13, 1995.
414. Ibid., April 12, 1998.
415. Ibid.
416. *Indianapolis News*, April 13, 1998.
417. Associated Press, April 14, 1998.
418. *Jackson Hole* (WY) *News*, April 15, 1998.
419. *Jackson Hole Guide*, April 22, 1998.
420. Ibid.
421. *Jackson Hole News*, April 15, 1998.
422. *Indianapolis Star*, May 1, 1998.
423. *Jackson Hole News*, July 29, 1998.
424. *Indianapolis Star*, February 26, 1999.
425. Ibid., May 15, 1999.
426. *Jackson Hole News & Guide*, June 23, 2004.
427. *Indianapolis Star*, March 17, 1998.
428. *Detroit Free-Press*, June 8, 1999.
429. Ibid.
430. *Tampa Tribune*, June 9, 1999.
431. *Detroit Free-Press*, June 8, 1999.
432. *Times of Northwest Indiana*, February 3, 1995.
433. Ibid.; February 4, 1995.
434. Ibid., February 4, 1995.
435. Ibid.
436. *Tampa Bay Times*, April 18, 2001.
437. *Dayton Daily News*, March 17, 2019.

ABOUT THE AUTHOR

Andrew E. Stoner, PhD, is an Indiana native and author of *Notorious 92: Indiana's Most Heinous Murders* and *Wicked Indianapolis*, along with other true crime, biography and political history books. Stoner, a graduate of Franklin College of Indiana, Ball State University and Colorado State University, is a former newspaper reporter and civilian PIO for the Indianapolis Police Department. He is an associate professor of communication studies at California State University, Sacramento.